THE FEARLESS MARKETING BIBLE FOR LIFE COACHES

SIMONE SEOL

FRECKLED BRILLIANCE PUBLISHING

CONTENTS

AUTHENTICITY AND INTEGRITY

FEARLESS MARKETING
PHILOSOPHY

STOP MARKETING

Stop "marketing."

Start telling the truth.

And leave people in a better place than when you found them.

THE BIGGEST SECRET

One of the biggest "success secrets" when it comes to social media marketing that nobody talks about is to actually give a shit about the people around you.

Treating them like humans, not "prospects" who might give you money if only you could nail down your copy.

Connecting out of the sheer enjoyment of connecting with another human being, not to "network."

Asking, "How could I be useful to this person?" before you think about self-interest.

Even when — or especially when — there seems to be no potential for self-interest.

Saying hi, offering a kind word — just because it's a nice thing to do.

Just what I call "good human-ing."

How can you bring more of it to your world today?

FEARLESS MARKETING IN A NUTSHELL

Show up. Be a person.

Be interested in other people more than you're thinking about yourself.

Listen deeply and connect to people's hearts and intentions.

Say hello.

Be thoughtful and kind.

Be more generous than you need to be.

Offer to help in any way and in any context where you can be useful to another.

Tell people what you do over and over and over again.

YOUR NEXT CLIENT

Your next client is 100% already in your orbit.

Speak to them today from where you are.

3 SACRED ASSUMPTIONS

I downloaded these ideas a while ago and they have been the cornerstone of how I show up on Facebook.

They have really served me well and I'm delighted to share them with you.

What would happen if you just assumed, without the need for prior evidence, that:

1. I love people.
Variations:
I like people.
Everyone is different, but I can find something I like about everyone.
I have something to offer.

2. People love me.
Variations:
People like me.
I am welcome here.
I am invited here.
There is something valuable here for me.

3. Facebook is a party.

And I get to decide how I show up and what kind of experience I have.

Did you know that if you believe things intentionally, you start to create evidence that they're true?

Circumstance: I'm on Facebook

Thought you can have on purpose: I love people

Feelings that the thought produces: Open, curious, generous

Actions you're likely to take from that feeling: Add kind comments to others' posts, share generously and openly

Result: Warm interaction that creates more love

So fun!

3 RULES OF SHARING

Before you post, ask yourself:

1. Is it loving?
2. Is it true?
3. Will it help at least one person?

LOVE MORE THAN YOU FEAR

Your mission today, should you choose to accept it, is to love your people more than you're anxious about being accepted.

SHOW YOUR FACE

If you're hiding your face from social media, you're hiding your uniqueness.

How the hell are peeps supposed to get to know, like, trust, and pay you when they literally can't even see your glorious face?

They can't. Even if they want to.

You are literally pushing money away.

If you do have some pictures of your face, but if they're blurry or from 8 years ago or otherwise *not* representative of what you actually look like today — same thing.

It's like trying to find the love of your life on an online dating website with a cat meme for a profile pic.

It won't get you what you want! I don't care how awesome your words are.

Show your exquisite face.

BEARER OF MEDICINE

If marketing feels like a heavy and un-fun obligation to you, it's only because you are temporarily disconnected from the reality in which you are the bearer of medicine in a world full of people in pain.

SELLING REFRAME

What I thought selling was when I hated it and was afraid of it: duping someone into giving me money

What I now think selling is, now that I fucking love it and could do it all day: having belief in my offer, deeply understanding and loving another person, and serving as the bridge between where they are now and where they want to go

GIVE THEM A TRANSFORMATION

People pay you to help them when they are powerfully convinced that you can help them get a transformation.

The best way to convince someone that you can help them get a transformation is *not* by telling them in fancy words and strategies that you can (what most people try to do), but by actually demonstrating it.

As in helping them get a transformation, like, now.

Marketing is nothing but helping people get transformations for free.

The better you get at it, the more business you'll have.

MARKETING IS SOCIAL CHANGE

Marketing is the first way you effect positive change in the world.

Your marketing *is* the social movement you want to lead.

Don't wait until someone signs with you to do good in the world.

All the things you want to help your clients do? You do it before they even sign with you through your marketing.

Your marketing *is* social change.

Here's your challenge for today:

Fill in this sentence.

When my best client is done working with me and gets the transformation they came for, they feel _____, _____, and _____.

The three blanks?

That's what you're here for. That's what you want to create more of in the world. That's what you *can* start creating more of in the world, today.

You know what that starts with?

You.

Feel _____, _____, and _____ first, and your marketing is already working.

WHAT TO GIVE AWAY

My policy on what to "give away" and what to hold back?

I give away everything, and I hold nothing back.

(In terms of ideas and value. Not time or products, obviously!)

Not only that, I give the best.

From the top of my intelligence, whenever I can. The newest and sharpest ideas I have.

How are people supposed to know I can help them if I keep my most helpful ideas to myself?

Some people have a fear that if they give away too much for free, people won't want to pay them.

I have found it to be the opposite.

The best way to make money is to demonstrate clearly what results you get people, and show your brain/product to be *the* asset that can help to create those results.

When you give away free stuff that actually creates awesome results, that is the best advertisement anyone could have.

Plus — business is just more fun that way. Generosity just feels so good.

My mentor has a policy: "I want meeting me to feel like winning the lottery." What an awesome thought!

When people feel that way about you, money will be easy, don't you think?

People also worry if they give away all the ideas, they will run out.

I am infamous for my potty analogy: "You need to poop it all out before you can poop again!"

There is an infinite reservoir of amazing ideas.

The more you practice tapping into it and sharing the results, the better your new ideas will get.

WHAT THE GAME IS REALLY ABOUT

The game is not about external markers of business success or money, though it might seem like it.

The game is doing hard things so we can grow into the full creative capacity of our souls.

EVERYONE IS YOUR ALLY

Assume everyone is your ally, even — especially — when your brain insists on the opposite.

Everyone is either here to make you feel good or to help you to learn and grow.

Without the former, life would be sour. Without the latter, there would be stagnation.

That's why everyone is your ally. They are here for your thriving.

When challenging situations come up with these assumptions, ask yourself:

- If there is a nugget of truth in what the other person is saying or doing, what would it be?
- How would Love respond?
- What would it be like in this situation to assume good intentions?
- If this person loves me and I love them, how would I act?
- If a benevolent universe sent me precisely THIS person today to help me to grow into exactly who I need to be, what can I learn?

PEOPLE HAVE MONEY

Did you know that if you *only* sold to the top 1% of the wealthy English-speaking countries (USA, Canada, Australia, UK), that's 3.6 million people?

Think you can find a couple of them to give you money this month?

LOVING YOUR BUSINESS ON PURPOSE

Falling in love with your business, letting yourself be seduced by it, is a hell of a lot easier than "working on your belief."

LOVING THEM ON PURPOSE

What would happen if you believed: *I love people*?

When you scroll through your feed, imagine how you would interact with each post if you were to just assume that you love people.

It doesn't mean you have to agree with everyone. It doesn't mean that you want to invite everybody over for dinner.

Love is different than liking or agreeing with. Love is appreciating their humanity. Love is appreciating the fact that we're on this Earth together, moving through life at the same time. Love is appreciating that life could be hard for everybody.

And everyone is just doing their best.

Can you have love for them on a human to human level?

REMEMBER YOU'RE LOVED

Whenever you think *social media is stressful,* you are forgetting how much everyone loves you... whether they know it or not.

EVERYONE PAYS YOU

EVERYONE is your client.

When you show up believing that, miraculously everyone pays you.

Some pay you money.

Others pay you in:

- goodwill
- referrals
- allowing you to gain experience helping another person, which sharpens your skill and broadens your perspective
- the gratification, the warm-and-fuzzies of knowing that you're making a difference in a way they'll be paying forward

Show up. Serve. And get paid.

Every single day.

JUST ONE PERSON

What if your job in marketing was helping to change ONE person's world at a time, instead of chasing more "engagement" and bigger "audiences"?

If you believed that it truly comes from serving ONE person at a time, and being truly present with them and loving them the best you could, what would you do differently?

As the quote goes, "Helping one person may not change the world, but it may change the world for one person."

MARKETING IS A PARTY

What if marketing = throwing the best party for your favorite people?

THERE ARE NO HATERS

What if there are no "haters"?

There are just people who are confused or who have temporarily lost access to their Love Center.

THE NEW SOCIAL MEDIA THOUGHTS

Common thought: Social media is a show-off contest.

We say: No, it's where we can go to find our common humanity.

———

Common thought: Social media is toxic and a waste of time.

We say: No, social media asks each of us to bring a vision of the world that we want to create, and to experiment with creating that first in our own corners.

———

Common thought: Social media is not "real life."

We say: No, people find friends, love, shop, gossip, find causes, connect, fight, start movements, idle, teach, learn, work, network, have sex, and create on social media. That is literally LIFE. And it's real.

———

Common thought: Social media is all smoke and mirrors.

We say: No, not if we aren't afraid to be REAL with each other. We are each responsible for bringing the realness and speaking truth to illusions.

The rules of intentional, enlivening, loving, courageous, world-saving social media marketing aren't already written.

We are writing them.

HOW TO GET THEM TO ENGAGE

How do you get audiences to engage with your marketing?

Stop thinking of them as "audiences" whose "engagement" you need.

Start thinking of them as human beings for whom you have a chance to make a positive difference today.

YOU ARE A HELPER

You are a helper.

Because of that, every time you show up, you end up helping.

It's not your job to know exactly whom or how.

DON'T PERFORM "EXPERT"

The most powerful leaders I know don't perform "expert."

They don't stand on a pedestal, lecturing at the rest of us. They don't only ever show up in a suit, with rehearsed lines and a whitened smile.

When they talk, they don't talk in expert-ese.

They remind you of your own humanity, but a bigger version of it.

They teach and inspire by example how to inhabit the *fullness* of life — including the dark and messy stuff — with more trust, love, and courage than you thought possible.

Those are my role models.

HOW TO SHOW UP SUSTAINABLY

I get this question a lot. And here's how I invite you to think about things:

How would you feel if you were dating someone you were really into and they said:

"I'm wondering how to show up to this relationship sustainably. I've done the blaze-and-fizzle thing too often before. Should we calendar our dates? How far in advance, how much space in between would be good for me to not lose interest in you, I wonder...??"

It would suck, right?

People ask how to make it sustainable when they think, "I give input with the expectation/hopes of adequate output."

What if you chose thoughts that make it a relationship that you were excited to be in, and excited to nurture?

The dating metaphor again:

If you're excited and gratified to be in a relationship with someone whom you adore, you wouldn't be thinking, "Okay, I have to show up X amount of times, in this particular way, for them to keep liking me."

Showing up in itself would be a joy. Giving to them freely, finding ways to make their lives better, to see them happy would be, in itself, the reward.

When I was dating my now-husband, I knew exactly when I was going to see him for the next few months. Because we were both busy people, we knew each other's schedules and we made plans accordingly.

Planning helped me to create the right container for the joy and thrill of being with him when I had so many other things going on.

But that planning-and-strategizing is in service of the relationship, as opposed to, "Ugh, how many times do we have to meet, how do I have to put out for you to keep giving me what I want?"

Is that difference clear?

You can love being on social media for its own sake.

Just because you love your friends and enjoy hanging out with them.

And it gives you joy to serve them in all the ways you can.

That's how I create that joy, that love, that enjoyment — with the thoughts I choose about the neutral circumstance of social media and the humans that are in it.

THINK HIGHLY OF COACHING

The more highly you think of life coaching as a profession, the more effective your marketing will be.

We make dead fucking serious change in the world.

We make dead fucking serious money.

Don't forget it.

STAY IN THE MIRACLE

No one forced us at gunpoint to start a coaching business. The opportunity to speak our voice freely, positively impact others, *and* make money is the privilege of a lifetime.

Stay in the miracle.

BEYOND SOLUTION-PEDDLING

As life coaches, we're not here to just be solution-peddlers.

Though being a peddler of an awesome solution is fucking awesome.

Solving problems is sacred. Creating better solutions and selling them is also sacred.

And also, if you're a life coach, you are also a purveyor of wisdom.

The solution is *what to do.*

The wisdom is *why it matters.*

The solution is *here's the best path from A to B.*

The wisdom is *how to carry yourself on that journey from A to B.*

Spend time mining for and rooting yourself in your own wisdom.

And when it gets way, way bigger than the technicalities of the *solution,* lean in.

YOUR OBLIGATION

As a life coach, it is your obligation to dream bigger for yourself *and* for your client.

To stretch your vision of what's possible for yourself *and* for your client.

And to deliberately be with the discomfort of believing in something that has no basis in reality.

To deliberately sit with the doubting, shaming gremlins in your brain who ask, "Are you stupid or something?"

For you *and* for them.

To learn how to effectively speak comfort and possibility to those fears.

Creating bigger dreams and making ideas become reality — that is literally our job.

That is why we have the best job in the world.

Step up to yours.

Make it bigger.

YOU DON'T NEED A PROGRAM

Here's the #1 thing you don't need as a coach:

A program.

So many people have been taught that they need some kind of plan — an outlined program, a curriculum, a syllabus, a thing that says, "Here's part one, part two, part three — see? I know what I'm doing!" — to qualify to help people.

This is not true.

You can just show up and coach.

That is enough. Enough to create *all* the results for our clients.

The value of coaching doesn't come from the *program*. It comes from the coaching conversation.

The most impactful thing you can ever experience is the back-and-forth with another human being who sees you already in your wholeness.

That is the gift.

That changes lives.

That is the best bang for anyone's buck.

Don't forget it.

IF I WERE STARTING OVER

So I asked myself, *What would I do if I were starting over?*

If I had no platform. No reputation. No followers. No expertise honed over years of experience.

If I were freshly trained, eager but with very little experience, and with no one willing to pay me a cent to coach them.

In other words, where I was nearly a decade ago.

Here's what I would do if I were starting over, knowing what I know now:

1. I would pick a very specific, tangible result I could help people get — something that people already want.

Not because I'm trying to establish a niche. But because I want it to be easy for people to volunteer to be coached by me.

It's a lot easier for people to say yes to "I will help you eat less sugar" than "I will help you be true to your inner compass."

And I would recruit as many people as possible to say yes to free coaching.

2. I would invest in my marketing and sales skills, knowing that being a good coach is a completely different skill set than growing a business.

I would use those skills to find people, make offers to help them for free, and make it easy for them to say yes to me.

I would also use those skills to start building up a social media presence as a coach.

3. I would spend as much of my time as possible coaching people for free, knowing that with each hour logged, I am growing in skill, confidence, and professionalism. So, even if I'm not making money right away, I'm still getting paid in intangibles.

I would keep coaching for free until I have enough experience that I *know* for a fact that my skills are worth $100/hour.

By that point, it will no longer be a guessing or hoping thing for me, because I will already have success stories, testimonials, and a confidence I can feel in my bones.

At that point, some of my free clients will be offering to pay to work with me. Others will be bringing in referrals. I will start charging $100, because I know I can get them results worth that much.

I would create more clients by continuing to show up actively in person and online, and telling the world about what I do and how I can help.

This is the most secure, most logical, and most authentic path from zero to *paid*.

Knowing what I know now, if I could have a do-over, this is what I would do.

CALLING PEOPLE OUT

Good marketing calls people out.

Good coaching calls people out.

And a common misconception here about *calling out*?

It is *not*: "You're doing it wrong, so let me school you."

It is: "I love you. Your higher self has a different perspective on this. Let my higher self conspire with your higher self to remind you."

COURAGE AND PURPOSE

DECADES TO COME

What values will sustain your business not just for the months, but the years and *decades* to come?

YOU MAKE IT GOOD

You make social media a better place every time you show up.

It doesn't even matter what you say.

Who you are is good for the world.

SELF-BELIEF NOT NECESSARY

You don't need perfect self-belief.

You just need a nugget of courage.

What will you do with a nugget of courage today?

GLAD TO SEE YOU

I really like your face and am glad to see you pop up on my feed every time.

What if you believed that this is what your followers say to themselves every time you post?

I BELIEVE IN YOU

I believe in you.

Not in a fluffy, feel-good, "you-go-girl" way.

But I know that you have something inside you that can help others.

In a way that can change their lives.

I know the lies of smallness and scarcity that your brain tells you.

Because I have the same brain. We all do. It's called being human.

But I believe that you're capable of experiencing the suck and not dying and learning from it.

I believe that you are capable of choosing that, over and over.

I believe that you have the capacity to grow.

Not overnight. Not even necessarily elegantly.

(That's not how I grew.)

But I do believe that you want to and that you will.

When you do this enough (and I believe you will), success is inevitable.

That's why I believe that you'll get what you came for.

DON'T SHOW UP FOR TODAY

There's someone whose life is going to be changed in 10 years because you bothered to show up today.

I think about this all the time.

Because you kept going today, you're going to come up with your own groundbreaking methodology 2 years from now, which one day is going to save the life of someone who is not even born yet.

Because you kept going today, the muses are going to drop on you the idea for your career-defining book in 3 years from now that you are going to finish writing 5 years from now.

Because you kept going today, someone is going to tell their friend about you. That friend is going to start following you silently, not making a peep for another 7 years, when they will finally get in touch and decide to hire you for the biggest contract you've had yet.

It's mind-boggling to think about.

Don't show up for today.

Show up for the future.

Show up for the countless faces of people who don't even know you exist yet, who will come into your life at a different point of evolution and be changed for it.

Show up for those who are and will be silently following you.

Show up for those who aren't even born yet.

Don't fall for the limitation of *what is*.

It's an illusion!

COMPARE AND DESPAIR

Compare and despair only happens because you're forgetting the inevitability of who you are becoming.

NO ONE LIKE YOU

So what if someone else offers the same thing?

There is absolutely no one in the world with your specific combination of personal history, experience, knowledge, personality, energy, skills, and talents.

Hence, even if someone else technically offers "the same thing" as you, it will feel like an entirely different experience from the clients' end.

And there are clients who will resonate madly with you *because* of who you are *being*, not because of the specific features and benefits of what you offer.

In that way, you are completely original and incomparable, no matter what you choose to do.

SELF-COACHING IN MOMENTS OF VULNERABILITY

In marketing, my brain often offers me the thought:

That was too pushy.

You shouldn't have said it like that.

That comment makes you look like a total weirdo.

You come across so smug.

You should have told the story differently.

And other forms of *you are doing it wrong, you ARE wrong, and nobody likes you.*

Here's how I coach myself right in those moments:

That may be. But that was the truth of how I was thinking at the moment. And that is always enough because I am enough, exactly the way I am.

TAKE THE FOCUS OFF OF YOU

Every single one of us became life coaches because we wanted to help.

Your mind drama will disappear the minute you take the focus off *you* and put it on those who are suffering in silence right now because they don't know where to find help.

HAVE YOUR OWN BACK

Have your own back. That's the place where you can be the kindest, most generous version of yourself. (And that is *mission critical* for marketing.)

NO SUCH THING AS BEHIND

There is no such thing as *behind*. You come to things when you come to things.

If you're reading this now, it's the perfect time to try something new. There is no expiration date on any of the ideas contained within this book.

They are always available to you and *for* you.

Jump in whenever, with whatever.

KIND THOUGHTS

Put yourself on a steady diet of kind thoughts about yourself.

Because your brain sure as hell ain't gonna serve them up on its own. (Your brain means well. Blame it on evolution.)

Lately, I am training my brain to think kind and affirming thoughts about myself that are unrelated to work or other conventional measures of worth.

Like:

- I am a great daughter.
- I am a super wife, so much fun to be married to!
- I am a great sister and an even greater dog aunt.
- I am a good citizen (I yield subway seats to the elderly, I pick up litter when I can, etc.)
- I have a great imagination!
- I love my own smile. It's BIG!
- It's easy for me to see the beauty in small things and I really like that about myself.
- I would be really useful to have around in the event of a nuclear apocalypse because I can make a good meal out of any unlikely combination of ingredients.

What about you?

Why is this important and relevant to marketing?

Try being someone who feels terrible about herself in general and tries to find validation in business.

Eeeeeek. Painful and not profitable.

DECIDE TO BELIEVE IN YOUR GOODNESS

Maybe one of the most important internal shifts I made was deciding to believe in my own goodness.

And *deciding* was not a one-and-done deal, but a muscle I've had to strengthen for over a period of time.

I had to practice liking myself even when I acted against my own values, even when I acted from anger or desperation, or even when I fell into *that* old, shitty pattern that I thought I was done with forever.

Even in those moments, I had to practice believing that my existence was inherently good, that my breath was welcome here on earth, and that my "flaws" were not things to be overcome or fixed or transcended or smoothed over, but were allowed and loved as part of the mystery of being alive as a human being.

It's not always easy. It takes re-commitment every day.

But I am so grateful to those who taught me — and modeled for me — how it is an option for me to have my own back no matter what.

YOU ARE A REMINDER OF WHAT'S
POSSIBLE

Who you are, as you are, in this moment, is a reminder to your people of what's possible.

How is this true for you?

ENOUGH

Repeat after me:

Who I am now is enough.

What I know now is enough.

WHOM I know now is enough.

There is always enough for me.

SAFE TO TRUST

Repeat after me:

It is now safe for me to be seen.

It is now safe for me to say what I really mean.

It is now safe for me to trust my truth with people.

THE TRUTH OF WHO YOU ARE

Here is a thought to get rid of vulnerability hangover or shame about what you already posted, especially when you find your brain babysitting reactions (or lack thereof) to it:

What I wrote was true of who I was being at the time of writing. That has value, because the truth of who I am has value.

THE SAFEST THING

Taking risks is actually the safest thing you can do when hiding is slowly draining life from your soul.

HOW TO MAKE PROGRESS WHEN YOU FEEL LIKE GARBAGE

You don't need a big, impressive goal if the thought of that stresses you out.

If other people's big, impressive goals make you feel pressured and less-than, I say, FUCK THAT SHIT! You get to move on your own timeline! It is your sovereign right!

To get moving, all you need a teeny tiny miniature, *I suppose it's not entirely impossible that I could make that happen...* milestone.

Your brain will ask, *What's the point? That doesn't even count for anything.*

That's okay. It means you have a healthy human brain, which reflexively kicks up objections and fears when you try to do something new because it evolved to try to keep things as same as possible to maximize the odds of survival in Neanderthal days.

But it's 2020 now. There is no hungry tiger outside the cave. You are not in imminent danger of death (although you're totally allowed to FEEL like you are!)

You can comfort that fear, reminding it, *I know it feels like we should be making a hundred-mile leap at once or it doesn't count. But that's okay. It's not all or nothing, we're just trying something different. We're okay. Whatever happens is okay. I love you anyway.*

And do the teeny tiny thing.

Yeah?

Let yourself have that teeny tiny accomplishment!

And allow yourself 10 seconds of celebration. (No more necessary!) Give yourself a high five.

What you're after is a hit of dopamine — the neurotransmitter that gives us that reward-and-pleasure feeling, crucial to learning and habit formation, which makes us chase the next "high." That makes us want to chase the next learning.

Let that good feeling gently carry you to the next tiny thing. That's how we make forward movement when the world feels so heavy.

There is nothing wrong with you.

You got this.

TAXES YOU PAY

All the *no* consults are the taxes you pay in advance for your inevitable success.

CREATE AN EVIDENCE FILE

For the first couple years of my business, I had a notebook of testimonials or even nice words people said about me and my work.

Not just coaching, but art, writing, general thoughts about me — *anything*.

I printed them out and pasted them all.

I never missed a kind word someone said. They were all in the notebook.

And I had to make myself read them every single day.

Before every client session.

Often, out loud to myself.

Because my brain told me persistently that I didn't know what I was doing and that I was a fraud and was worthless, it was the only way I could make myself remember that who I was and what I did was valuable.

I am only effortlessly confident now because I put in the work of actively building the muscles of self-belief.

I clung to that notebook for dear life. So now, I no longer have to. It's just all automatic in my brain.

I literally copied and pasted that shit with scissors and glue.

That's what it took.

We all need this kind of reinforcement. None of us gets to transcend having an asshole human brain.

How can you give more of that reinforcement to yourself?

YOU DON'T NEED TO BE PERFECT

This is just a reminder that you don't need *perfect strategic words* to get someone to want to commit to you, whether it's love or coaching.

ON YOUR WAY

On your way to figure out confidence, you'll have public face-flops.

On your way to figure out selling with integrity, you'll act greedy and desperate.

On your way to figure out copywriting, you'll be overwrought and boring.

On your way to figuring out how to be excellent at what you do, some people will witness you being less than that.

It's not a sign that you're doing it wrong.

It's actually a sign that you're doing it exactly right.

It is literally how we learn all the things worth learning.

Non-linear. Messy. Wobbly.

So much "failure" that builds those fibers of the new muscle you're building.

You're nailing it.

Keep going.

LET THEM SEE YOU IMPERFECT

Because it means you're showing up as someone who is brave and secure enough with herself to learn and grow in the public eye.

And that is SO admirable and enviable to so many who have brilliant visions but feel hobbled by their own fears of not being enough.

WHAT YOU KNOW IS VALUABLE

For those who feel like they're too deep in their own shit to coach other people, if your imposter syndrome is running the show, please remember this:

You know you're miserable because your default fear-thoughts are being triggered by your primal brain.

Most people in the world have zero awareness of their own brains.

Zero skill of identifying thoughts and emotions as separate from themselves.

You're in a river of unavoidable human discomfort.

They're in an ocean of suffering born of preventable and educable ignorance.

Ignorance, *not* that they're stupid.

But they haven't had the luck of encountering what you now know and take for granted.

You've been there before, before you found coaching.

I have.

It's fucking terrible being trapped inside your fear and thinking that you ARE your fear, never having encountered the idea that it could be otherwise.

It's the *worst* place to be.

And you can help them get out of there.

You are a life coach, even when you feel terrible.

Even when you've been feeling terrible for weeks, or even months.

What you know is valuable.

Your skills are valuable.

You. Are. Valuable.

GETTING IT WRONG IS REQUISITE

Getting it wrong 10,000 times is requisite for having a kick-ass business. You might as well have fun with it!

SO MUCH CLOSER THAN YOU THINK

You are so much closer to being fully booked than you think.

Even if you only have 2 clients now. Even if you get tripped up talking about your offer, every time.

You might *think* you're so far away. You might think there is so much fear to get over, so much more experience to have, so much more confidence you need first, so much thought work to do, so many more people to reach.

But — I swear to you.

The gap truly isn't so big. You are one or two powerful shifts away. One or two habits away.

That's all it takes.

YOUR PEOPLE

MONEY THOUGHT

Who I am already is perfect for my dream client, and I don't have to know exactly who that is before I write.

PEOPLE LIKE YOUR FACE

You don't have to be available to debate with, appease, cajole, convince, or console those who aren't interested in assuming the best of you.

Plenty of people like your face. Plenty of people think highly of you *just because*. They will hear whatever you have to say in good faith because it wouldn't occur to them to do otherwise.

Those are your people.

STOP EXPLAINING YOURSELF

How would your marketing change if you put a hard stop to explaining yourself to people who are committed to misunderstanding you? (Even if that explaining is only happening in your head.)

1.5 BILLION ENGLISH SPEAKERS

How many people do you need to sell to next year to make the money you want? 20? 40? 100?

Actually do the math.

I bet it's not that many people.

Consider that there are almost 1.5 billion English speakers on earth.

That means you have 1.5 billion opportunities to make the money you want. Most of them ARE on the internet.

Go find your people.

SPEAK TO THOSE ALREADY SOLD ON YOU

Many people won't give you the benefit of the doubt.

They'll want you to prove yourself.

Defend your methodology.

Justify why you decided X and not Y.

You'll feel on edge around them, even as you concede that they have a point.

And they aren't your people.

They're not bad people. They mean well (sometimes). You might even love them.

And they're not whom your business is meant to serve at this moment.

Your Right People are out there.

The ones you're meant to serve.

There are enough of them that you can have a profitable business.

Your Right People will already have been *sold*.

If not on a particular product, then on the idea of *you*.

No defending or justifying or proving needed.

They will take it for granted that whatever you choose has excellent reasons behind it.

They'll support and admire your decisions even if they don't *get* it 100%.

Their only questions will be, "How can I get more?" and "Where do I sign up?"

Here's the twist:

It's not your job to know exactly who those people are or to go out and look for them.

Your only job is to trust that they already exist — in spades — in your existing orbit.

And to speak to them and serve them only.

WHAT SOME WILL JUDGE YOU FOR

What some people judge you for is exactly what some other people will want to pay you for.

Let it out.

DECIDE THAT THEY GET YOU AND LOVE YOU

You can market fearlessly when you believe you're speaking to an audience that *gets* you and adores you.

(Hint: You can always decide that you are.)

IGNORE THE "YEAH, BUT" PEOPLE

There's a really big difference between listening to people who love you and conversing with an open heart, and engaging with every rando who has zero interest in genuine co-discovery of truth, eager to come at you with a ready-made dismissive attitude of "yeah, but" to whatever you say.

The perfect response to the latter is *no response*.

(Plus delete/block when necessary.)

You get to take care of you first.

It's not selfish to constrain your attention to those who want to communicate lovingly, even in disagreement.

HOW TO TREAT YOUR COMMUNITY

Remember that you are entitled to NOTHING.

Okay, that was a bit harsh to start with. But it can actually be such a relief to remember this! It can save you so much anxiety.

Remember: people in your group are *not* there to serve you, your ego, and your business interests. You are there to serve *them*.

You are not entitled to their attention. You are not entitled to their "engagement." You are not entitled to having them jump at your offers.

Everything they might give you must be earned through the value you give, with devotion, earnest heart of service, and consistency.

Remember: it's like a romantic relationship. You can't show up for dates only when you feel good and expect them to think you're great and be loyal to you.

Show up and serve when you think nobody's following. Show up and serve when you feel discouraged by the lack of "results." Never stop innovating and playing with new ideas.

Always expect to give more than you get back.

The members of your group are there because you made an offer to make their lives better. So, ask yourself every single day, "How can I make their lives better?"

If you spend time with that question and implement the ideas you come up with every day, you'll end up with an amazing group that the members constantly thank you for in no time.

HOW TO RUN A GREAT FACEBOOK
GROUP (OR ANY GROUP)

You do not need a group to make money. It is never, ever a requirement.

I know lots and lots of rich business owners, including successful coaches, who don't have a Facebook group. Many are not even on Facebook! So: 100% unnecessary.

Second, if you're struggling to create resonance and get clients now, a group will not change that. In no way will a group make it easier for you to sell.

Work on your beliefs and energy first. Have the confidence that you can create resonance and clients first, and then you can leverage that in a group.

Third, if you start a group, assume you will need to nurture it actively, consistently, and treat it like an unpaid part-time job for a full year.

This is true of anything brand new you start, whether it's a YouTube channel, a podcast, or a Facebook group. It needs time to grow and become something. Time to go from fetus to fully-formed and functional adult.

None of the tactics above is a magic solution that suddenly helps you get more sales.

In fact, they create more work, more busyness, and more confusion if you're trying to use it to solve the wrong problem.

Ask yourself: if it will take me a full year of unpaid work, is it still worth it?

Of course, you might actually see the return sooner than that.

But the assumption of *no money for a year* will keep you in the right energy. It will keep you detached, lighthearted, and in the spirit of service.

I believe my business has benefited from my Facebook group ONLY because I am incredibly unattached to it being a money-maker for me.

I already know how to make money. I already know how to get eyeballs on my stuff.

I run my group only because it is so fun for me. It is like a lab for my creative ideas.

It delights me to *give back* because I got soooo much value for free from super generous teachers when I was starting out.

And plus, I get to hang out with the coolest people.

So. Much. Fun.

If I get clients from it, it's just the cherry on top of the cake. That is 100% my mindset.

It might sound like I'm talking you out of starting a group. But I am so not.

I am talking you out of starting a group for the wrong reasons, out of sequence, which will create unnecessary work and confusion for you later.

If you dream of creating a vibrant community centered around your ideas and offerings, let's make it happen.

But first, learn how to market and sell without it.

Then your group will be fucking EPIC.

BEST PRACTICES FOR RUNNING ONLINE GROUPS

You know what makes my group so high-value?

And why engagement is through the roof and people keep inviting their friends, even though I barely promote it?

This isn't for me to toot my own horn.

It's because I'm obsessed with analyzing and documenting what works. When I know what works and share it, success becomes follow-able and replicable for everyone.

There are very specific things I do, which I believe are responsible for my group's success:

1. I pretend that everyone is a paying client.
2. I make very clear what the goal is for everyone (better marketing, more clients), and I hold myself to the standard of helping everyone create that.
3. Whoever is feeling stuck and not seeing progress, I pretend that it's my "fault."
4. I pretend it's my obligation to see that every single person gets breakthroughs in ways that are pragmatic and measurable.
5. I pretend that my reputation depends on the *results* people get from being in my group.

Note: I didn't say, "My reputation depends on how much fun people have, how inspired they are, or how warm-and-fuzzy and confident they feel."

I'm focused on results.

You're either landing consults and signing clients... or not.

It's a brutal, clear-cut, no-room-for-negotiation binary.

If you're *not*, I hold myself personally responsible.

This has me asking every single day:

- Everyone who is not getting big results — why aren't they? (Here, assuming the problem is never the group member but 100% the way I'm showing up and teaching.)
- How is this teaching landing?
- If I keep saying the same thing over and over and people aren't receiving it, how should I try saying it differently?
- How can they get better results?
- What is the most effective way to communicate X?
- How can I make it simpler?
- How can I make it more fun?
- How is everyone feeling and how can I help them feel more of the useful emotions? (Loved, loving, powerful, open, creative, curious, resourceful, etc.)
- How can I keep raising the bar?

If you have a group, you should be asking yourself the same questions.

If you keep this up, I guarantee that your group will also be so high-value that it becomes a movement on its own — and you'll get all the clients you want from it.

ENTITLED

Entitlement shows up like, "I should be as successful as she is."

"This should have gotten more attention."

"I *should* be further along."

Everyone agrees entitlement is bad. But being entitled doesn't make you a bad person.

It's not a character flaw. It doesn't even mean you want something without having earned it.

What it *does* mean is that you are temporarily disconnected from your power as a creator.

This happens a lot for sensitive people for whom the world feels like a lot — too much. And a lot feels out of their hands because they spend more time than the average person processing incoming stimuli.

This happens also for people who are not necessarily more sensitive but who have been affected by trauma. So naturally, it is more difficult to feel in control when you are healing from something big and overwhelming that happened to you.

When people learn how to process the world with more safety, and when people heal their trauma, they naturally feel more power.

The power to belong to one's own life story.

The power to create something out of nothing.

The power to change that which is outside of you.

When people gain more personal power, entitlement naturally becomes a thing of the past.

MAKING OFFERS

WHY YOU SHOULD MAKE AN OFFER

You don't make an offer because you're sure people are going to buy that day.

You make an offer because someone out there needs what you have today.

They might need to hear it 2, 5, or 25 times before they say yes.

But the whole time, they were thinking about it.

And you were on their mind because you kept showing up and reminding them of what is possible.

WHY THEY DON'T WANT YOUR FREE THING

The reason people aren't:

- taking advantage of free coaching you offer
- hopping on the free webinar you offer
- signing up to download your freebie
- joining your free group

...is NOT that "you suuuuuuck."

(Sound familiar, anyone?)

Why does this happen? We tend to think people operate based on money.

"Since coaching is expensive and nobody has money, they'll for sure want the free version!" is the assumption.

But, as we can see, this isn't quite true.

Think about it. If you had a choice of going on a date with either one of two people, and:

- A wants to take you out to a fancy restaurant that costs $150 per head
- B wants to take you to a low-key but cool pizza place that's $20 a head...

...would you automatically choose A just because it's more $$$ that YOU end up not having to spend?

Probably not, right?

What does your gut say? Who seems like you'd have a better time talking to? Getting it on with?

Who is cuter? Where is each person from?

Who has a better-fit personality? Better taste in music and books? Politics better aligned with yours?

You'd be weighing sooooo many other things besides how much dinner will cost.

What if it's the same thing in marketing?

What if free or how much money is one of the last things someone considers?

You could be the most eligible bachelor(ette) in all the lands, but if you don't learn how to talk about WHO you are and what you've got in a way that makes the right person go, "Ohhh, that is for me!", you might be spending all your evenings alone.

How to do this:

Communicate that you are available (remember, you're so hot that people might just assume you're already taken).

Say things in a very straightforward way — that means telling people exactly what you offer in very simple, direct, plainspoken words so there is no room for ambiguity or confusion. Say it in the way that an 8-year-old would understand.

Give them a taste of what it'll be like to go on a "date" with you by being the real you, not the weird stilted "expert" version of you, and by speaking the way you'd speak to your friends over brunch, letting your personality quirks and idiosyncrasies shine.

For every marketing conundrum, if you understand why something is happening, the fix is simple.

If you're not getting enough "bites" on your offer, free or paid, always be experimenting with the above 3 points.

Don't expect to nail it right away.

Garbage it up the whole time. Use your courage, not your *gotta get it right* perfectionism.

Gather data points.

I promise you'll start seeing different results.

HOW TO MAKE OFFERS THAT AREN'T AWKWARD

In so many ways, business is analogous to dating.

You and your person get to know each other little bit by little bit. You invite them closer incrementally, creating space for a little sexy push and pull. The more they get to know you, the closer they want to come.

Starts with a coffee...
a polite museum date...
followed by dinner...
taking walks together...
more dinners...
you meet their pet...
go on weekend outings...
then you might have the "okay, we're a couple" conversation.

Sure, you might skip a few steps. You might *know* right away... but your game plan wouldn't necessarily be to ask them to move in on the first date.

All that brings me to: what is the offer that you currently have? What are the ways you bring people closer to you? Are you doing the equivalent of asking someone to move in after a first date?

If so, what things can you build in so that there are more ways to get to know you and fall in love with you incrementally?

If a free call is all that you have to offer, make no mistake — those calls are actually very intimate. It's an hour of just you and them on the phone or over video. You wouldn't do that with just anyone, right? It's a big commitment in terms of time and trust and energy.

You probably want an in-between step between you and consults. Ways for you to get to know each other. Ways for you to give value and opportunities for people to find out what it would be like to "be with you."

That's why I'm a big fan of having an email relationship with my people. (i.e. *list-building*, though I kinda hate that term.) That's why I invite people to follow me on Instagram and invite them to actually talk to me via DM. That's why I provide tons of help for free.

I create freebies (like e-books), occasionally do free coaching, and organize free trainings and challenges (like my Facebook group) so people can "go on dates with me" before making the Big Commitment.

By the way, it's not true that someone always *needs* all the in-between steps. (Some people do decide to get married on the first or second dates! It's true!)

It's most definitely *not* the case that "the more in-between steps you have, the better." I think just one or two in-between steps between you and the consult is enough.

I'm also definitely not saying, "You should have a group and an email list like me." In fact, I had a good business long before I started my Facebook group, and I know so many people who are doing very well without an email list.

There is no formula. You have to create your thing. Start where you are. Try something.

Ideas for what you can invite people to before asking them to "move in" with you:

- Watch your video
- Listen to your podcast
- Join your email list
- Follow you on Instagram
- Send you a private message or "comment below" as an end in itself
- Free bite-size thing
- Read your blog post

The only requirement is that you do it out of true love and a desire to serve, and a desire for other people to get to know you — not from a place of "this strategy worked for [person X] so it must work for me, too."

What in-between "dates" are you offering your people?

P.S. This also solves the problem of "it feels weird to offer the same thing over and over again."

THE FUNCTION OF AN OFFER

The function of an offer is to help someone get what *they* want. It has nothing to do with you getting *your* needs met.

WRITE BETTER INVITES TO CONSULTS

If you always get confused about how exactly to word the part of the copy where you invite people to the consult call, the problem isn't your writing skills.

The problem is the lack of clarity in your own mind.

It will help hugely to answer these two questions for yourself.

1. Who exactly is the kind of person who needs to be on this call?

Hint: It's not everyone. It's not even everyone in your niche.

Look back on your own past. Were you always ready to invest in coaching? I bet not.

Think about the kind of people you want on the call. What kind of attitude do they have?

What kind of people would actually benefit from being on the call? Where is their brain at now? What pushes them to the precipice of change?

The more specific you get about this, the better. This way, you know who the hell you're writing TO. So much fuzziness happens because you don't actually know who you're writing to.

2. If they get on the call, what's in it for them?

How is this for *them*?

You have to be very clear with yourself how the call is for them, regardless of whether they decide to work with you or not.

If you think of the call as purely for you to *get a client*, you will struggle with this, because you will fail to sell the free call authentically from a place of service.

If you think that this call is only useful to them for them to realize they need you, that will put you in a *convince-y* place, which is also not a powerful place to sell from.

You need to do some work in your own mind to sell yourself on why this is a fantastic opportunity for the client regardless of the outcome.

Bottom line: if you know exactly who you're talking to, and you know exactly how what you're offering is good for *them*, it's easy to know what to say.

Get clarity on all of this first, and the rest is just details.

DON'T OUTSOURCE AFFIRMATION

What if it were up to *you* to believe that you are liked and valued? That your stuff is worth buying?

No one is responsible for affirming that for you.

Remember, if you lean on *engagement* to affirm that stuff, not only will you not sell very much, you won't have much fun being on social media.

(Let's face it. Fun is the entire point — at least it is for me.)

People will be turned off by the energy of anxiety and desperation. If you've ever had that energy (I'm raising my hand first here — I've had that energy a lot and I'm sure I still do sometimes because I'm human!), I want you to know why people are turned off by that.

It's not because there's something flawed and shameful about you.

It's because when you are believing the thought *my work is not worthy without their approval,* the rest of us can intuitively sense the untruth of that, and we are all wired to move toward truth and away from untruth.

To be sure, seeking approval and validation is a very normal, healthy, and understandable human desire. We can give ourselves plenty of compassion and understanding for having a normal primate brain!

But let's be aware of when fear is driving the bus. I think love is a much better driver.

By all means, promote your stuff. Brag. Tell us about your business. Reach out, connect, and sell.

But do this from a place of joyful sharing, knowing that your ideas and your presence matter because you decided so.

SAY IT AGAIN

You know the thing you assume everyone already knows because you've already told them so many times?

They don't.

Say it again.

Say what you think is obvious. Again.

Assume only 10% of interested people catch you each time you say it.

Assume that even those people need to be reminded 8 times before things click in their brains and they take action.

DON'T BREAK UP WITH THEM NOW

Launching something, writing a few offers, and being disappointed no one bought is like going on a few dates and being disappointed they didn't propose!

Don't break up with them *now*. That would just make you a fuckin' weirdo!

They're just about to fall in love! Keep showing up and courting them.

CALLS TO ACTION

There are lots of ways to be really thoughtful about issuing calls to action.

That's something that you can play with.

- What if I say it this way? What if I say it that way?
- What if I try to entice them this way? Does that work?
- What if I try to entice them that way? Does that work?
- How can I create safety? Can I try this? Can I try that?

Please keep in mind that the whole point of experimentation is that you don't know for certain in advance if it's going to work out the exact way you intend.

If you knew, it wouldn't be called an experiment. It's really important to let half of the experiments "fail."

All failure is just feedback and learning, and it's taking you closer to your inevitable success.

HOW TO MAKE OFFERS
UNAPOLOGETICALLY

I have so many clients and colleagues who tell me, "I don't know how to make offers."

Well, you *do* know how to make offers.

You might not yet have figured out how to do it without feeling pushy, sales-y, sleazy, or intrusive.

The good news is that the ease and confidence you're after involves just a simple mindset switch.

Here it is:

If you approach offers as "I need you to please buy X from me and give me money, please?", that's going to feel bad for *you*, and it's going to feel bad for *them.*

The weird feeling that people get from selling comes from this idea that you are beholden to them.

That you're on the helpless receiving end of someone's decision.

Eeeek! Who wants that, right?

Listen. It's the opposite.

Imagine you're on a busy street on a nice sunny day, and out of nowhere, it suddenly starts raining like crazy. A torrential down-pour. Everyone is freaking out and scrambling.

Then someone shows up with an armful of umbrellas for sale.

Everyone is like, "Oh my God, thank God!!"

You're the umbrella person. You feel me?

You are the one that can get them dry.

You are the one with power.

You are the one bringing the thing they want.

You are the generous one extending an invitation.

Do you feel the difference?

I am the one with the solution.

If you're used to thinking of yourself as being the one "in need," it might feel weird and foreign at first to step into that energy.

That will change the more you practice intentionally feeling being the *person with the umbrella.*

If you know exactly what your *umbrella* is and you know exactly what *rain* is pouring on your people, you will never stop being able to make offers confidently, easily, and joyfully.

Because when you *know* that what you have can help them, making an offer becomes a generous act of service.

IT CAN'T WAIT

You have a powerful message to spread, and it cannot wait.

GO DO THE THING

Feeling a roller coaster of crazy emotions?

No?

Then you're under-marketing.

Go and challenge yourself to DO the thing!

THOUGHTS ABOUT UNSUBSCRIBES

Our brains want to make unsubscribes a bad thing. They want to convince us that this is middle school all over again, and you've just been rejected by the popular girls.

Well, guess what, brain? This ain't middle school. This is business. And making cash is way fucking better than getting to sit with Brittany and Amanda at lunch.

My philosophy on unsubscribes is that if you're not getting a lot of them all the time, it's because of one or more of four reasons:

1. You're not adding enough new people to your list consistently.
2. You're not sending enough emails so people aren't saying "no," but they also don't know your business exists.
3. You're not being your undiluted, unedited, unique self. You're presenting like a mayonnaise sandwich instead of the spicy parsley falafel-stuffed pita that you are.
4. You're not making enough powerful offers. People aren't opting out of what you have. But they're *not* opting in in a way that matters either.

Creating unsubscribes means you're showing up, offering value, and letting other people actually know who the fuck you are.

Creating unsubscribes is also a form of self-love. When it happens, you know you're creating more space for those who are a *fuck yes* on you.

WHOM YOU'RE MARKETING FOR

You're not just marketing for the people who'll buy this week. You're marketing for clients who will want to say yes next month, 3 months later, or a year later.

A LOT OF PEOPLE READY TO BUY

There are a lot of calm people in the world, right now. There are a lot of people who have plenty of money they love to spend on solutions, right now.

Go make a damn offer.

OFFER AS AN ACT OF ALTRUISM

Make every offer an act of altruism.

Humans are altruistic. Altruism always feels good.

If you don't genuinely believe that your offer will benefit the other party more than it benefits you, you should either work on your beliefs or find something else to sell.

Never sell anything that benefits you more than it benefits them.

When [the value they get out of it] exceeds [what you get in return], offering is easy.

Think of how fun it is to give a thoughtful gift.

Feeling conflicted about selling is most likely a sign that you need to work on this part of it.

ANGEL OF POSSIBILITY

You, life coach, are an angel of possibility.

Sprinkle that angel dust around.

THERE'S ONE PERSON

Repeat to yourself every day:

"There is *one* person out there who has been following me and is talking themselves into hiring me and is looking for a sign, a reason to feel safe enough to say yes today."

OF COURSE IT SHOULD INCLUDE AN OFFER

Don't waste your brain space debating whether an email should include an offer. Of course it should.

No over-explaining, preciousness, no hedging. No pretending that it's an imposition. No pretending that you're running a charity, or an expensive hobby.

You're in *business*. That means you sell things. They give you money. You give them a high-value transformation and an amazing return on their investment.

There is no room in this transaction for apologies.

Ain't no selling ever happens without offers. Put them in every damn email.

Do it in the body. Do it in the P.S. Do it everywhere. Do it every day.

If they don't want to hear your offers, they aren't your ideal clients anyway. Love them and let them unsubscribe. Everything else is you wasting your own time and people-pleasing them.

That results in no money and no clients for you, and no transformation for anybody.

Might as well just fold up shop.

THE POINT ISN'T TO GET CLIENTS RIGHT AWAY

The point of making frequent offers is not to get clients right away.

When we believe that, we look for the validation of immediate results or needing people to "bite" before we feel like we're allowed to keep going.

We get discouraged super fast, super easily, and get sucked into that start-stop-start-stop cycle.

What if the point of making frequent offers was to get practice making offers?

Making an offer is a skill, and you get better the more you do it.

Another sneaky benefit of making offers all the time is that it allows you to gather data points for making more effective offers over a period of time.

The effects of making offers a lot is cumulative over time.

Here is a simple example of a good offer:

"I am throwing a party. There will be great music and your favorite food — Indian snacks! I cannot imagine it being the same without your energy, wit, and stylishness. Would you please come join us?"

This offer is an ode to both the vision of what you want the party to be *and* who you believe the invitee to be.

Even if they decline:

- They are elevated by your vision and intention.
- They are reminded of who they are at their best, and that their presence is valued.
- You have opened a door to a new, desirable experience for them.
- You leave them better for having heard the offer, even if they don't say yes.

This is what happens in a Good Offer. (This only works if you mean what you say. Let's just always mean what we say.)

IF YOU DON'T LOVE IT

Do you love your offer?

If so, why?

If not, why not?

So many marketing questions and dilemmas you have and get stuck on can be traced back to when you're not in love with your offer.

It can be fixed when you're willing to find your way back to love.

Either change the offer so it's easily lovable or change your thoughts about it.

TAKE ADVANTAGE OF PEOPLE'S PAIN

I take advantage of people's pain just so I can sell them on a greater vision for their lives and what they know deep in their souls about who they are and what they're capable of.

The next time someone accuses you of it, own it.

WHEN NOBODY SAYS YES

When you write an offer with big hopes and don't get any takers, an **early stage entrepreneur** thinks:

Oh noooo. Nobody wants it. Nobody wants me. Why do I even bother? I probably shouldn't have come off so strong. My copy sucks. I wonder if I should take that down. I'm so embarrassed. Maybe I should change my offer.

A **mature entrepreneur** thinks:

They all just leaned in a bit more, already talking themselves into it. Nice. That's one down, fifteen more to go this month. What aspect of this can I play with differently next time?

You can think like an advanced stage entrepreneur no matter where you are, just because you decide to.

GETTING OUT OF YOUR OWN WAY

DOING IT ANYWAY

All my results come *not* from dramatic accomplishments, but from questioning my mind when it says, *Eh, it's probably not worth it,* or *Nahhh, that's unnecessary!* to little things... and then doing it anyway.

I STILL HAVE TO WORK ON IT

I'm the queen of fearless showing-up-ness, and I always have to work on it, because my default brain pattern fills me with fear. Yes, even now.

I'm a queen of dishing out love-soaked hard coaching, and I always have to work on it, because my default brain wants to go to frustration and resentment and stay there. Yes, even now.

What are you making it mean that YOU "still" have to work on it?

TAKE CARE OF YOU

YOU are your business's most valuable asset.

Your brain. Your bod. Your spirit.

Your well-being is literally the most important precondition for your long-term profitability.

Please. Protect your assets.

There's a fabulous word my client Jennie Juechter coined —"YES-ergy." It's exactly what it sounds like.

The energy of YESSSSS.

From that comes all good things.

What we want. What we want to pay for.

Please tune into it for the rest of us.

CELEBRATING

Whenever someone has a win, I celebrate wildly, then always ask, "What was the thought that created that?" or "What did you do that worked?"

That's because you cannot create bigger success without taking total responsibility for and being a student of your existing success.

We tend to zip by past successes.

We're uncomfortable with celebrating ourselves, and even more uncomfortable with studying it.

Something in how we've been taught makes us feel like it's arrogant to look at it too closely. But actually, not doing so might be costing you future success.

If you don't make a habit of owning, studying, and celebrating what you've done well, your brain will tell you "that was a fluke."

Your brain will tell you, "This is hard!" and "You don't know how to do this!" even when you have *literally just done it.*

Why feel like a randomly lucky beneficiary or a helpless victim of external circumstances when what you are is a powerful creator?

Celebrate away!

STEALING MONEY FROM THE FUTURE

Every day you show up halfway or not at all, you're stealing money from Future You.

ASSUMING NOBODY'S LISTENING

What if every time you assume *nobody's listening*, you are dead wrong?

And every time you assume *nobody's interested,* you are also dead wrong... and you don't get to find out unless you keep going?

SO WHAT IF YOU FEEL TERRIBLE?

Under-booked coach brain:

I feel trouble. That means my offer / niche / copy / energy / audience must be wrong. Ugh. What do I do? I need to change it. But how? Oh! A podcast!

Fully-booked coach brain:

I feel terrible. Of course I feel terrible, I'm growing. It's not a problem. Let me get curious and get some work done anyway.

Get yourself a fully-booked coach brain.

You'll be thinking at a different level that makes being fully booked inevitable.

WOULD YOU TELL YOUR DAUGHTER?

Would you tell your daughter (or niece, or beloved child in your life):

"You're so pretty, but your nose is too wide."

Or: "You're so smart, except you suck at math."

Or: "You're so sweet, except none of the popular girls like you at school."

No?

Are you sure?

So why on earth are you telling yourself:

"People are engaging with my posts, but nobody is reaching out for a consult."

Or: "I have two clients, but I haven't had a new one in a while."

Or: "I had 10 consults, but only signed 1 of them."

WHY? Why why whyyyyy would you say that? How does it help you?

You mutter, "But it's true," just like you're reporting the news.

But as we can see watching the difference between CNN and FOX, there are a lot of ways to report the news.

You can "report the news" like an asshole. Or you can "report the news" in a useful way that actually helps. (I'm not endorsing or disparaging any one news outlet, just mentioning two of the most famous. We can all agree that there are definitely ways to report the news like an asshole.)

Stop reporting your own news like an asshole. Start to tell yourself better stories, because they're going to directly shape what results you get in your business next.

Tell yourself your strengths. Remind yourself where you're learning and expanding. Report on what's going right. Document where you're grateful.

There are enough of those stories to fill the day, I promise.

SLEAZY AND SALES-Y

There are people who think I'm sleazy and sales-y. I don't make it a problem. I consider it part of being in a real business instead of a hobby — allowing for the discomfort of people having thoughts about you that you don't like.

NOT GETTING THE RESULTS YOU WANT

If you think that you *don't have the results you want in your business* and it feels 100% true and you're ready to fight anyone who wants to argue otherwise, remember:

The minute you think this thought, here's what your brain's mechanism for cognition and learning does:

- filters only for stories that prove it true
- deletes evidence to the contrary
- distorts neutral evidence to fit the existing thought
- gets you feeling emotions and taking action that creates *further* proof of the thought

So, of *course* it feels true.

If you want it to keep being true, go on believing that thought.

If you don't, consider the possibility that your current *reality* is just a simulation-projection of your thought programming.

Make a different fucking choice about what sentence you want to feed it next.

THERE'S NO SUCH THING AS PUSHY

What if *pushy* is not a thing?

What if your *pushy-meter* is kinda broken because of *good girl syndrome*?

What if the only way to truly be pushy is if you genuinely don't give a shit about the other person?

(And that is *never* you.)

THERE IS NO SPAMMING

You are not a SPAM-human.

Therefore, it is IMPOSSIBLE for you to spam someone.

It is NOT a thing.

It could not happen if you TRIED.

THERE IS NO OVERSHARING

What if "oversharing" is not a thing?

A novelist friend of mine, highly respected in the literary world, griped to me that when men write about their personal lives, it's considered fascinating.

When women write about their personal lives, it's trivialized as "domestic" literature, less than "serious."

Like, "Aww, how cute, all the ladies with their little stories about their little lives."

Remember the 3 Rules of Sharing?

It must be:

1. Loving
2. True
3. Useful to at least one person

Nowhere on that list is, "It's the right amount of revealing."

What's oversharing to one person is powerful and life-saving to another.

Keep sharing "too much" — from love, truth, and a spirit of service.

YOU'RE CLOSER THAN YOU THINK

Hey, if you felt terrible and kept going and showing up today anyway, you are a rockstar and I am rooting for you so hard!

Don't stop!

You're closer than you think!

I HAD TO FAIL 1,000 TIMES

In order to learn how to write precisely to the reader's psychology, I had to write and publish copy that failed at that objective 1,000 times.

In order to learn how to write to be succinct and punchy, I had to write and publish copy that was wordy and boring 1,000 times.

In order to learn how to write to be super compelling, I had to write and publish copy that fell flat 1,000 times.

In order to learn how to write sales copy with integrity and conviction, I had to write and publish copy that felt sales-y and pushy and insecure 1,000 times.

You're nailing it.

Keep up the work.

And no whining.

This is the path we've chosen because we can't imagine anything more worthy.

It's a privilege to be able to grow into our dream selves.

THEY HAVEN'T EVEN MET YOU YET

Consider that 99% of your future clients have not even met you yet.

So, will you pretend everyone knows your entire life story and is bored with it already, or will you speak as though you're meeting fresh pairs of ears, ready to fall in love with you and your message?

IT'S NOT YOUR NICHE'S JOB

It's not your niche's job to make you feel warm and fuzzy and confident.

It's *your* job to *love* it, cultivate belief in it, create evidence for its value, and *sell* other people on it.

BEING HIRED WITHOUT A NICHE

Each minute you spend worrying about your niche is one minute you could have used to create clients instead.

You know what gets people hiring a coach without regard for a niche?

When they like you and trust you to help them.

They think, "Damn, that woman is smart and she gets where I'm at right now. She kinda seems like she's not full of shit. I like her. Maybe she can help me."

Making it any more complicated than that is just drama.

NICHE DRAMA

There's a difference between working on clarifying and evolving your niche and indulging in niche drama.

The former is a normal and healthy part of business growth. It involves taking action and pivoting, with productive learning in each step.

The latter is a waste-of-time business-killer.

Being in drama means you *stop* working and being useful to people because you're too busy grinding your wheels in direction-less, momentum-free confusion.

We all need to stop it.

You know what it means for you to have niche drama? It means you're in a state of *I don't know how to help people.*

If you have been trained as a life coach and you think you don't know how to help people, your problem goes way, way beyond marketing strategy.

No one who knows how to help people just sits and stares at the wall. Because there is *so much need* in the world.

If you haven't noticed, people everywhere are suffering. In subtle ways, big ways, sometimes gargantuan ways.

We need life coaches who know that they can show up and help everywhere, in every way. If they're not sure what to do, they will try something. If they're not sure exactly what kind of help someone needs, they'll be busy figuring it out.

They will keep noticing where people are hurting, and they will step up to help. It literally does not fucking matter exactly where. Hurting people are everywhere.

Life coaches are helpers. We are here to reduce suffering and add more connection, love, wholeness, and thriving in the world.

Every single coach here has the skills to help anyone with that, on any given day. And when you do that, that is called marketing.

On any day you're NOT doing that, you're bailing on not just your business, but your vocation.

Nailing down the world's most perfect niche custom-designed for your brain and the zeitgeist is none of your fucking business.

Getting up every day, paying attention to humans around you because you give a shit, helping them, and continuing to learn and iterate on how to *better* help because you care more about being useful to other humans than being perfect — that is your business.

When you do that, inevitably niche clarity follows.

No more niche confusion.

Be where you are, use what you have, and do what you can to HELP.

Today. Tomorrow. And every day after.

You'll have a real solid goddamn life coaching business for as long as you want.

WHAT SELLS INSTEAD OF A NICHE

If you're not selling, your brain might tell you it's because you don't have a clear enough niche.

I am the living example that niches are unnecessary. I made close to six figures without any niche whatsoever.

I can name 5 other successful entrepreneurs off the top of my head who did the same. And that's not including actual famous people. (Like, what the heck is Byron Katie's niche?)

Here's the catch, though:

You don't need a niche, but you do need to know exactly what kind of people you serve.

So, who is that for you?

If you can't answer immediately, *specifically and clearly*, that means you are confused — for now — about whom you are serving.

This means your people are confused about whether your offer is for them.

Confused seller = confused audience = no sale

No bueno, right?

But here's the good news. This can change. And you don't have to wait to consult with an *expert*!

The answer is inside you, and you just have to be willing to do a little bit of digging into who you are, and have the chutzpah to decide.

Specifically and clearly doesn't mean some kind of super-narrow niche.

No, no, no.

Though I didn't have a niche, it was always clear to me *what kind of people* I was serving.

As for me? My people were:

> Smart, irreverent, slightly wacky people who wanted to change a specific habit through rewiring the brain

I spoke to *them* very clearly by:

- talking about the brain a lot
- dispelling common ideas about how long it takes to change and how complicated the whole deal is
- just being my usual direct, curse-y, idiosyncratic self with the weirdness turned all the way up

This is as much of an issue of exclusion as inclusion (i.e. knowing whom you're attracting vs. whom you're repelling).

For example, by showing up with all of my personality, I *filtered out* people who weren't into my potty mouth and straight-talkin' style. I *filtered out* people who wanted to talk about their childhoods for hours and hours. I *filtered out* people who weren't ready and eager to roll up their sleeves and get to work.

In conclusion: clarity about whom you are serving is not the same thing as having a niche.

You don't need the latter.

You absolutely need the former to sell.

CLIENT-CREATING THINKING

90% OF WORKING ON MARKETING

90% of working on marketing is managing your own emotions. Only 10% is the actions you take.

You don't have to feel amazing or positive or *in belief*. You only have to be WILLING to feel *anything*.

DON'T SELL THEM ON YOU

Don't sell them on how great you are, or how great coaching is, or what a great deal your package is.

They don't care about any of those things.

Sell them on them. Their desire. Their future. Their capability. Their worthiness.

They care about all of that. *A lot.*

ENJOY THE RIDE

To become an accountant who can be hired by firms, you need a 4-year degree.

Law school takes 3 years.

Medical school takes 4 years and then more years of residency.

Most brick-and-mortar businesses take several years before they even break even.

Yet, for some mysterious reason, people expect to achieve marketing and sales mastery overnight.

It makes no sense, right?

Slow down.

Enjoy the ride.

Savor the learning.

It's worth it.

You'll progress a whole lot faster if you're not beating yourself with a whole bunch of *not good enough* and *not fast enough* judgments.

FUN TO BE MARKETED TO

Intentional thought: *It's so fun to be marketed to.*

When you believe this about *your* marketing, you'll become a marketing machine.

YOU CAN THINK IN TWO WAYS

You can think:

Copy is so haaaaaard!

or *Bridging the gap is so haaaaard!*

or *Showing up imperfectly is so haaaaaard!*

or *Being consistent is so haaaaard!*

Or you can think, *Every day, I'm building money-making neural pathways that are going to pay me back for the rest of my life.*

Same challenge. Same work. Different spotlight.

What would you rather choose?

IT'S NOT ABOUT THEM

The fastest way to be in client-creating energy?

Be in your own breakthrough. It's got nothing to do with convincing *them,* and everything to do with surprising *yourself* with what you can do.

HOW TO CREATE CONSISTENCY

Consistency is never the problem.

It's got little to do with the lack of discipline or your work ethic, either. Trust me, you're hard-working enough.

Inconsistency is only ever the symptom of how you are thinking about your business. It is a symptom of the relationship you have with it, as if it were a person with needs.

Imagine having a baby, and saying, "I struggle to feed the baby consistently."

Ummm. That would never happen, right?

I don't care how "lazy" you are. You wouldn't even consider it an option not to feed your hungry baby, if you had the means, no matter how tired or annoyed or unenthusiastic you feel about the task. Because keeping the baby alive and healthy isn't optional.

The only reason you're not consistent is that taking care of your business-baby still feels optional to you. This is not a problem or something to judge yourself about.

Instead, we can be curious and redirect our brains.

What about your business doesn't feel optional because it matters so much to you? Is it helping people? Being able to speak to people exactly where you were when you were suffering, and having the ability to make a difference? Growing into a braver, more loving version of yourself? Is it even the money that you want to make?

Once you find what does feel like a *no matter what* thing, what if it's enough to focus on just that?

That's how you generate consistency.

WHAT GRIPES YOUR ASS?

I created this concept called The GMA List. GMA stands for "gripes my ass."

If you're a life coach, you KNOW there are things around you that, when you watch them happen, you're like:

"NOOOOOOOOO!!! That shit gripes my ass! Grinds my gear! Kills my groove! Waters my sandwich! This is NOT happening on my watch!"

If you're me, it's when a talented, golden-hearted powerhouse of a coach decides to quit business because they were one or two brain tweaks away from making real money and their brain was screaming at them, "It's taking too long, you don't have what it takes," and it's so scary, they give up.

If you're a weight and body love coach, it might be when you see a woman utter to herself, "Ughhh, I look disgusting," before spending $189 on another "Hollywood juice fast."

If you're a midlife reinvention coach, it might be when you see someone put up with a cheating, aloof asshole of a partner because they think, "I'm already 52... no one will ever find me attractive again."

If you're a home-magicking coach, it might be when someone looks at their giant pile of memorabilia and feels deep shame that

Marie Kondo would have them throw it all out, but they can't bring themselves to do it, and then concludes it must mean they're a slob and a loser.

What is it that, when you see it around you, makes you so mad and riled up that the sheer anger is enough to bust whatever self-doubt you have?

It gets you leaping off the couch and into action to try to intervene because this shit cannot go on, and if I'm not gonna help, *who will*?

The more specific and detailed your GMA list, the more you're in touch with the big WHY that animates your business.

And when you write about it? Copy gold. Because you're speaking to the person right where they find themselves.

I'm always intentionally collecting my GMAs. You should be, too.

VICTIMHOOD IN MARKETING

Do you know what subtly kills your marketing? Victimhood.

Nobody thinks of themselves, *I am a victim.*

But they do think the following:

- I am being called out/attacked/insulted.
- Facebook just makes me feel _____.
- They're all ganging up against me.
- I feel judged by X.
- Y is always trying to pick a fight.
- Z always has to one-up me.
- I'm not liked here.
- I'm the odd one out.

Raise your hand if you've ever had any or all of these thoughts. Yeah, me too.

They feel terrible. Ew!

The good news is that they are optional. And we can have a different relationship with these thoughts once we have awareness into what they create.

Here is what these victimhood thoughts do:

The more you believe people are out to get you, betray you, call you out, or criticize you, the more you'll hide and self-censor.

Useful for telling the world about your genius?

No.

Thinking you are being attacked makes you feel constricted and small instead of expansive and powerful. This puts you in a fight-or-flight state, in which the creative and intelligent part of your brain literally shuts down.

Useful for coming up with great ideas and solutions?

Nope.

The more you believe someone is judging you, the more you judge them in return, and there is no room for curiosity or compassion in any of it.

In other words, you become a less loving, smaller version of yourself.

Does it help you to be an inspiring example for your clients? Does it look like a life coach walking the talk?

Methinks: hell to the no!

Be onto yourself. Notice where this is happening. And first be kind to yourself.

It's completely normal to feel like a victim. Your brain is not an asshole. It's just doing its job of trying to keep you alive and not get kicked out of the tribe!

You're also not a bad person or a bad coach because you have these experiences.

You are just human! Compassion for all the humans!!!

And ask yourself:

- It's possible I'm misunderstanding their intentions. It's possible I'm just defaulting to the most familiar story. What other interpretation is possible?
- How do I want to feel in this situation?
- What would it look like for me to extend grace to myself, and to them?
- What would Love do?
- What would Generosity do?
- How would I think about this if I believed this person was on my side?

DOESN'T NEED TO BE PERFECT

Thinking you need to write perfect copy to create clients is like thinking you need to say the perfect things to create a romantic partner.

Your ideal client *and* partner love who you *are*. As you are.

So: show them.

WHY YOU'RE STRUGGLING

You're not struggling because nobody's reaching out.

Nobody's reaching out because your brain says you're struggling and you believe it.

STOP BEING FASCINATED BY YOUR OWN BLOCKS

It could be imposter syndrome or perfectionism or fear of sales or self-doubt or difficulty with copy or whatever you think your "thing" is.

Your Big Issue.

The big dragon you think you have to slay.

People think about their block so much, dramatize it so much in their heads, endlessly analyze it, and picture themselves like heroes in an epic battle against a mortal enemy.

They ruminate on how long they've had it, how difficult it is to get out of it, and how defeated they feel against it every day.

Well, guess what?

Your block is not fascinating. There is nothing interesting or unique or complex about it. Your block is not special, and you are not special for having it.

It's really boring. It's really common. And its structure is quite simple.

Your "block" is no more than just a handful of sentences that your brain is used to saying in response to a circumstance.

It doesn't even know what it's saying. There is no *deeper meaning*. No existential significance.

But the brain keeps saying it over and over. Like a parrot. It's literally a reflex.

There is zero need to analyze it. There's no need to feel tragic about it.

All you have to do is to recognize that it's a thing that your brain is doing mechanically, and gently walk yourself over to another place in the brain where you think in a purposeful way.

Where your higher brain function can decide how you *want* to think and feel.

You practice that over and over. You let it get a little messy. But you keep at it. You get better at it.

And one day, the big bad dragon is just a lizard.

That's really all there is to it.

WHAT TO STOP RUMINATING OVER

A watched pot never boils.

There is NEVER EVER a good reason to spend even one second ruminating over your number of followers and number of "likes" and comments.

Strive to be more useful to people.

Push yourself to think higher-quality thoughts.

Love more, and listen harder to your Future Self.

You'll be surprised to see one day that your numbers have grown like crazy while you were too busy becoming excellent to notice.

TRY ALL THE THINGS

Try all the things to reach your clients.

You'll either be paid in money or in learning, which just adds to future money.

Either way, there is no way to lose.

BE ALGORITHM-PROOF

Think the algorithm is hiding your posts?

The questions you want to ask yourself are:

- How do I build a business that is algorithm-proof?
- How can I show up in a way that is so valuable people don't just consume me passively scrolling their feed? They *find* me. They *binge* me.

JUDGING OTHERS' MARKETING

Every time you cringe at or judge someone else's marketing as sleazy or desperate or boring or ineffective, guess what?

They're showing up, trying things, learning, failing, and gathering data.

Because of that, they're going to be more effective with each attempt.

When you're sitting there judging them, you are not going out and showing up and trying things and failing and learning and gathering data.

Your next attempt will not be more effective.

SELL YOURSELF FIRST

All the funnels and strategies and email sequences and Facebook ads and copy hacks won't save you if YOU are not sold on your own stuff.

If you are sold 100% on yourself as a coach, and on your offer — like, shout-it-from-the-rooftops, if-you-don't-buy-this-you're-stupid level of sold — you don't need any of that other stuff.

Sell yourself first.

STUDYING THE CLIENT'S MIND

Think back to when YOU hired your first coach:

- In order to hire your first coach at that point, what kind of dots did you need to connect for yourself first?
- What were the thoughts that took you from *contemplating hiring a coach* to *pulling the trigger*?
- What were things you needed to understand or believe first before you made the decision to invest?
- What were your own fears/objections that you overcame on your own before you reached out to the coach?
- What desires did you have that were inflamed, and what doubts did you have that were comforted?
- How?

Reflecting on these might help you connect with your ideal client in a different way.

NOT BELIEVING IN YOURSELF IS NOT INTERESTING

I hear so many people ask, "...but why can't I just believe in myself?"

And fondle that question on and on and on.

Here's the truth.

Not believing yourself is not interesting. It is not really worth analyzing or dissecting or digging into the depths of your childhood trauma.

It is not a permanent or intractable condition of your being, worthy of endless existential rumination.

It is simply every human brain's default "factory setting."

Of course you don't believe in yourself.

It doesn't take any effort or imagination to not believe in yourself. It's the easiest fall-back option.

The work that we do to grow and to become who we really want to be is to stake more in your imagination than in the "factory setting."

UNDER-BOOKED MARKETING VS. FULLY-BOOKED MARKETING

Under-booked marketing:

- Love me, save me, validate my business
- Chaotic, unpredictable, roller coaster of emotions
- Clients legitimize the offer
- I compromise and undervalue myself to get a sale
- My marketing is dictated by fear and scarcity

Fully-booked marketing:

- Learn from me, see me, join me in creating a better world
- Steady, consistent showing up
- Clients enhance what the offer already is
- I do the work to feel sufficient and sell from certainty
- My marketing runs on a spirit of service and love

UNDER-MARKETING

Most under-booked coaches under-market. And they don't even know it.

There are *two* main ways people under-market.

The first way is when people simply don't do enough of the right things.

People tell me all the time, "I just don't know *how* to get clients!!" But the funny thing is that they do know how.

And they're doing it.

Talk to people. Post on social media. Go live on social media. Write emails. Run trainings. These are all correct things. All of it WORKS.

It's just that they're not doing enough of it. It's kind of like wanting to run a marathon and running for 20 minutes diligently, every single day.

What they're doing is great. But it's not going to make them a marathoner.

If this is your problem, you need to multiply your marketing output by 3 times or 5 times.

And no, it doesn't take 3 times or 5 times more work or time. Not if you're using training your brain on purpose to create higher-quality content in less time.

Saying more with fewer words. Creating multiple ways to use the same ideas.

The second way people under-market is that they take a ton of action but they keep doing the same thing over and over that isn't creating the desired result.

That's kind of like wanting to get super fit and only doing bicep curls.

Like, you're going to get great arms, but what about the rest of your body?

To know what *else* to do that will make your marketing more effective, you need to stop doing, doing, doing, and look at where you're avoiding showing up. What emotional risks you're avoiding taking.

Maybe your real work is getting vulnerable enough and trusting that the right people will have your back when you tell more personal stories.

Or, maybe your real work is to let go of your perfectionism and be willing to be seen a little less scripted, less polished.

More human.

CEO THOUGHTS

The best brain is my brain.

While there's a lot in the external world that I don't have control over, I have 100% control over my thoughts, my emotions, my energy, my actions, and I take 100% responsibility for all of that and how I show up.

I create all the results in my business with my thoughts.

I always have the power to create new results by using my brain differently, by asking myself better questions, by having different thoughts, or by feeling different emotions. I am in control and I exercise that power to create results with a joyful sense of responsibility.

There is no one who knows my business better than me.

There is no one who can make better decisions for my business than me.

The best resource that my business could ever have is my brain and my heart.

DO NOT CROWDSOURCE ANSWERS

People ask questions in the form of:

- "Has .... ever happened to you?"
- "What would you do if ...?"
- "How many of you ...?"
- "Would you ... in this case?"

I call this crowdsourcing answers.

Sometimes, crowdsourcing is exactly the thing to do. Like when you're jonesing for the best guacamole recipe.

But more often than not, there are better alternatives. Because:

1. A crowdsourcing question is often masking a real question.

Looking within to find the real question often ends up being a lot more useful.

For example, "Has [something] ever happened to you?" might be masking "[something] happened to me. And here is the support I need to move forward."

Ask yourself, *what do you* really *want to know?*

Then state that plainly.

2. Give yourself permission.

A question like "Would you ... if ... ?" can mask, "Am I wrong for wanting to ... ?"

"Would you go with option A or B?" might be masking, "I want to go with A, but I'm afraid because ... "

"Can you help me think through this?"

What is it you wish someone would tell you?

What permission do you need?

What if you just decided and claimed that for yourself?

3. The greatest gifts can come from defying popular consensus.

Some of the best decisions in my life came from moments when crowdsourcing the answer would have unanimously put me on the opposite path.

Forget what other people would do.

What do *you* want to do?

Do you like your reason?

What would it be like to completely trust yourself?

DON'T ASK WHAT THEY WANT

"If I had asked people what they wanted, they would have said *faster horses*." — attributed to Henry Ford

Do not ask:

"Would you guys be interested if I ... ?"

Or: "If I offered X, would you sign up?"

Or: "What would you rather say yes to, offer A or offer B?"

You're not a pollster predicting the next election.

You're not a restaurant server asking the patron if they'd like to see the dessert menu.

You're a leader, a teacher, a coach.

It's your job to decide what they need and sell it to them.

YOU'RE RESPONSIBLE ON SOCIAL MEDIA

Rely on yourself, not the algorithm.

Instead of asking people to leave comments or GIFs to get Facebook to bump your post, learn how to think and write so powerfully and compellingly that they can't help but respond.

JEALOUS OF OTHERS' SUCCESS

Feeling jealous of others' success is a thought error. This is the same thought error our clients have when they're too scared to invest in coaching.

It's one that comes from making decisions from perceived limits of your present circumstances rather than the inevitability of your chosen future identity.

USEFUL VS. UNUSEFUL QUESTIONS

Useful questions to spend time on:

- How can I be more loving and generous today?
- What might be holding my people back, and how can I help them through it?
- What might be a blind spot for my peeps that would be useful for me to illuminate for them?
- How can I be more true to myself and my values today?
- If there is one person out there who needs what I have to offer today, who might be one word, one reminder, one story, one email away from saying *yes*, how would I show up?
- If I have everything I need to thrive today, how would I move forward?
- Who do I want to be in 3 years? Who am I becoming?
- What decisions would [Future Me] make about this?

Unuseful questions to spend time on:

- How many people liked my post?
- How come nobody responded to my offer from yesterday?
- How can I convince people to buy?
- Will doing X get me more followers?
- What is everyone else doing that I am missing?
- Why is this working for [other human] but not me?
- Why can't I figure out X?

BEST MARKETING QUESTION

Here's the best marketing question you could ask yourself:

If you held yourself personally responsible for moving your person (you know, the person who would be your ideal client) one increment closer to their goals today, what would you do?

Let's say there's a spy cam on them.

If it turns out they've moved one increment closer by the end of the day, you get $500.

And if they didn't, you lose $500.

What would you do?

NO "NEED TO"

There is no "I need to" or "I'll try to." That is the netherland where dreams DIE.

These statements say nothing except to communicate a lack of a decision.

What if there is no "need" ever? And there is no "trying" ever either?

You're either deciding and doing or re-committing to a previous decision and doing. Everything else is just your brain indulging itself.

Sometimes decisions take endless re-remembering and re-committing.

In fact, most worthy decisions do. That's okay.

Come back to deciding as often as you need to.

But no "I need to." No "I'll try."

THOUGHTS MASQUERADING AS FACTS

"Small audience" is a thought.

"Low engagement" is a thought.

They're never facts.

Notice how those thoughts make you feel.

NOTHING TO LOSE

Nothing will get you clients faster than when you believe you have nothing to lose and everything to give.

UNDER-BOOKED VS. FULLY-BOOKED COACH THINKING

Under-booked coach thinking:

- People need more information
- People are shopping around
- People are comparing features and benefits
- People make decisions based on price
- A bigger audience is better
- I need lots of buyers
- People don't have money
- I'm coaching to put out fires
- I'm competing with everyone in my niche
- I need people to buy so I can feel legit

Fully-booked coach thinking:

- People get enough information through who I am being
- People save up for it
- There's more demand than supply
- I want the right people, not a bigger # of people
- People make decisions based on quality and result
- Coaching allows people to become a different version of themselves (it goes beyond features and benefits)
- Less is more
- There is so much money to go around
- People love spending money on improving their lives
- I'm an expert, I know what I'm doing
- I have something that no other coach has
- I am a thought leader

WHEN YOU ADMIRE SOMEONE

When you see someone else showing up in a way you admire on social media, don't scroll by and think, "Well, that person clearly has some secret sauce."

Always assume that if you like it, you can do it, too. Not in a copycat way. You're not trying to mimic. But in a way where you are embodying the same qualities that makes someone else show up in an awesome way.

Ask yourself — what is that person doing that works? What is she thinking or assuming about her audience? About herself? What is she feeling? What are the textures of those feelings?

All forms of awesome can be learned. What if that were really true?

WHAT THEY WANT VS. WHAT THEY NEED

I was once asked, "Do you focus on giving potential clients what they *want* or what you *think they need*?"

My answer: all effective communication comes from meeting people where they are, business or not. Trying to understand *their* thoughts and emotions, and speaking in a way that will move *them*.

If you want a kid to stop throwing a tantrum...

If you want your husband to pick up the dry cleaning...

If you want your friend to agree to meet you at this restaurant instead of that restaurant...

...if you want to be effective, you'll have to speak in a way that *they* will resonate with.

When it comes to thinking about clients and how to speak to them, I ask:

- Who are my people? Who do I want to help?
- What are their hopes and dreams as *they* think of them?
- What are they experiencing as getting in the way? Why do they think they're struggling with this?
- How can I help them to feel safe moving one step closer to where they want to go?

If you train your brain to meet people where they are, you will be so much more effective in marketing — that is, compelling people to action.

SCARCITY MARKETING → CONFIDENT MARKETING

Scarcity marketing:

- Believing you're not good enough
- Showing up to social media looking for validation
- Messaging is timid and vague
- Copy comes across convince-y because you're trying to believe it yourself
- Start-stop-start-stop cycle

Confident marketing:

- Certain of your value
- Showing up to social media to serve and connect
- Messaging is inspiring
- Copy is compelling because you already believe it
- Consistently and purposefully showing up

This is a huge transition and is enough to get you making money.

A lot of what I teach is intended to get you to *confident*. You could create a nice following and earn a good amount of money if you know how to be in *confident*.

But if you're already there, and want to get to the NEXT level, read on...

INDULGENT MARKETING → SERVICE-BASED MARKETING

Indulgent marketing:

- Posting based on what's fun and interesting for you
- Making decisions based on what gets a lot of responses or what people say they love
- You love chatting with your fans

Service-based marketing:

- Focusing on *identifying and solving problems*
- Spending more time thinking about effectiveness than popularity
- Your marketing is actually creating measurable results in people's lives
- Messaging is not dependent on your mood and energy

WHAT EXCLUSIVE REALLY MEANS

Exclusivity is NOT about being fancy, better than other people, or generating fake scarcity.

It's about being very clear about whom you are best-suited to serve.

TOUGH BUT LOVING

I've had lots of people ask me, "You're tough *and* loving — how do you do it?"

Simple. I love you. And I don't need you to like me. I would *like* it if you liked me, but you don't have to have warm and fuzzy thoughts about me in order for me to keep loving you.

FAST AND FASTIDIOUS

There are two camps of marketers — I'm calling them the fast and the fastidious.

(As opposed to Fast and Furious. Geddit??)

You have different homework.

The fastidious:

This is 80% of people. This is you if you constantly second-guess and doubt yourself. You are slow to make progress because it takes you too long to write a post. You struggle to share. You worry about the rules and how to get it "right."

The fast:

This is 20% of people. This is you if you love sharing, have no problem putting content out there, and are quite prolific. But you keep getting the same results over and over again (low engagement and reach-outs) and you don't proactively learn or try new approaches. You keep doing the same thing and expect different results.

If you are "fastidious"— first, celebrate your conscientious nature! It's what makes you an excellent student and a highly-skilled and trustworthy coach.

Your medicine is: you must loosen up, take more risks, take action not to *get it right* but to get over yourself, and always be in the middle of your own garbage challenge. You must learn how to allow the discomfort of pushing things out onto the world, knowing you're not nailing it.

If you are "fast" — first, celebrate your sparkly nature! It's what makes you a badass innovator, and an inspirational leader and coach.

Your medicine is: you must slow down and have a (potentially emotionally intense) conversation with yourself about how you could be more intentional about speaking to people in a way that conveys your weight, authority, and efficacy (because you *do* have 'em!) and be willing to experiment with showing up differently to see what works.

HOW TO MARKET LOVINGLY AND CREATE CLIENTS

How do you market in a genuinely loving and authentic way?

Show up, connect, be thoughtful, create usefulness, and serve way more than seems reasonable, without expectation of return.

While you're doing that, how do you know you're actually also creating clients?

Put yourself in the path of discomfort on purpose by doing something that requires more confidence and faith than your brain says you have, every day.

I NEED TO WORK ON THAT

Never let yourself say, "I need to work on that," and walk away.

Always answer the question on the spot. Exactly *how* are you going to work on it?

How are you going to know whether you have worked on it and it's solved?

Otherwise, you're practicing lazy thinking, and cultivating the ability to get out of lazy thinking is exactly what creates clients.

DELETE "AFFORD"

Do the work to scrub the word "afford" out of your brain, forever.

Do you think crack addicts say, "I really want crack, but I just 'can't afford' it"?

No.

They rob and steal and turn tricks. Whatever it takes.

Why? They really, really, really want the crack. Like, really.

How we spend money is a reflection of what we prioritize.

If someone isn't spending money on you, they're prioritizing someone else.

And that's not a problem.

You can just get to work making your work more valuable or communicating your value better.

So much better than the "can't afford" story.

DECIDE, THEN FIGURE OUT THE MONEY

I don't decide what to invest in based on how much money I have.

I decide what to invest in based on what I think is the best in the market, because my dream deserves nothing less.

And I commit to figuring out the money.

If you hold this belief and walk the talk, so will your clients. They'll stop using money as a reason to not take you up on your offer.

There will not be money objections you can't overcome, because you radiate congruent belief.

NOBODY CARES IF IT'S FREE

Never emphasize that something is free as a selling point.

I see coaches doing this a lot. "It's free! It's free! You should definitely come get it because did I mention it's free?"

Something being free does not speak to its value.

I don't want your totaled 1994 Honda Civic, even if it's free.

A night at the Ritz, for free? Holy shit. Count me in.

Whatever your free offer is, present it like it's something that's worth paying real money for. (You better believe it, too.)

Why should they want it?

How would it help?

How is it exactly what they're looking for?

And by the time they get to the *free* part, let that information be a footnote and a pleasant surprise.

LUXURY EXPENSE

Saying that life coaching is a luxury expense is like saying preventive healthcare is a luxury expense.

THERE'S MONEY FOR COACHING

What if EVERY LAST PERSON ON EARTH had money for life coaching?

Think about it.

People pretend like coaching is a luxury expense and that there isn't that much disposable income to go around.

Think about the sheer scale of the alcohol industry. Or the global drug trade. Or the sex trade.

Actually, all of them taken together.

Legal and illegal.

Motherfucking gargantuan.

That's all the "disposable" money in the world funneled into temporary relief of the discomfort of being alive.

There is money to go around.

We take it for granted that huge sums will always be spent on temporary bandaging that usually only exacerbates the original problem and blinds us further to what really needs tending.

But we find it so hard to imagine that ALL that money could be used instead to develop and propagate *real* medicine that actually fucking works on life's pain (i.e. life coaching).

Not just *works on pain*, but sublimates, catalyzes, and alchemizes pain for the greater thriving of humanity.

What if?

And what if it's up to *us* to create that new reality?

CREATING VALUE THROUGH COPY

THE ONLY TWO RULES

Here are the only two rules of *content*:

1. Tell the truth
2. Say it with love

THE BEST KIND OF COPY

You know what's the *best* kind of copy?

Copy that's posted, published, and sent.

YOU MAKE MONEY EVERY TIME

Every time you publish copy, it makes you money.

When and how you get to "cash it in" is none of your business.

DON'T TREAT IT LIKE BOXES TO CHECK OFF

If you treat content creation as boxes to check off on your to-do list before you move on to more interesting things, your people will treat your content as things to scroll past to get to more interesting things.

HOW TO CREATE VALUE

How to create value? Believe that you — and the contents of your brain — have value.

How to create even more value? Strengthen that belief.

What if it actually is that simple?

So many of you try to solve this question of *how do I create value* from a place of doubt and confusion about your own value.

It does not work.

It starts here: *I have value. The contents of my brain are valuable.*

DON'T WORRY ABOUT ADDING VALUE

Don't worry about how to *add value*.

Be thrilled in your soul.

You'll be farting value.

GIVING VALUE EQUALS

- Being *useful* (This question will take you so far: "What do *I* find actually useful?")
- Leaving someone in a better place than you found them
- BEING the change you want to see in the world (Want more self-loving and empowered people in the world? You don't have to lecture at them to do it. *You* embody one — *you* show up as one — then they'll automatically follow suit.)
- Asking yourself, "How can I say it so it's simpler, smaller, easier to understand?"

DON'T LECTURE

Are you lecturing or sharing?

People's attention unconsciously drops off when they are being lectured to. Even if it's a nice lecture.

Which of the following makes your ears perk up more?

1. "Making your bed in the morning sets up your day for good feelings and success."
2. "For 37 years, I didn't make my bed. It seemed like a waste of time, until..."

For sure the second, right?

Most of us go into lecture mode when trying to write copy because we get into a weirdo "expert" performance mode.

We feel like we have to explain shit.

Don't do that. Nobody wants to feel like they're sitting in a classroom.

Instead, share from your life.

Be a human, instead of a weirdo "expert" person.

NO, THEY SHOULDN'T

Catch yourself every time you think:

They should *understand…*

What they need *to know is…*

If only *I could get them to see that…*

Check if there is a sort of anxious or eager emotion underlying that.

That's how you know you're in lecturing energy.

99% of copy I see flops because you're trying to teach, convince, or preach, instead of taking the reader on a journey, telling them a story, giving them an *experience,* or inspiring a feeling in their tummies.

Remember: nobody likes to be explained to. Nobody likes to be lectured to.

The unconscious mind instantly tunes that out. But it finds stories fascinating.

We like to follow the breadcrumbs of another human being's day-in-the-life.

We love to create our own meaning out of that.

NO THROAT-CLEARING

So you've written copy.

If it's a first draft, it contains a lot of throat clearing.

"Throat clearing" = the language equivalent of "ahem" where you're making noises but not actually saying anything.

"I've been thinking about this for a long time. The time has come, and I have decided..." → Just say what you decided.

"I'm excited to tell you that I am going to share what I learned from years of [blah blah]..." → Just say what you learned.

"It is my personal opinion that..." → Everyone knows it's your opinion, and opinions are, by definition, personal. Just say it.

Hey! Don't go into shaming yourself because you're like, *Oh crap, I've been doing it wrong.*

You're not taught this shit. Not in school, not at home, not at work. How were you supposed to know?

(Unless you're me and you got your writing ass kicked for *years*, being mentored by hard-ass grant writers and hundreds of thousands of dollars depended on you *not* throat-clearing.)

You're good.

Just start applying what makes sense and feels useful to you.

SIMPLE AND OBVIOUS

Just tell us what the hell you do, in very plain and brief language.

No elaboration needed.

In my mind, I'm constantly talking about being a life coach.

But you won't believe how many people message me and say, "I had no idea you do this."

DON'T SOUND LIKE A SELF-HELP BOOK

The vast majority of coaches who tell me they're struggling with getting business have this problem.

Read your copy — on your website, on your page, in your emails. Do you sound like a self-help book, or do you sound like you talk?

Do not sound like a self-help book.

Here's what sounding like a self-help book is like:

"Are you ready for a transformation? Finding your purpose can give you freedom and power. Give your inner self a voice, and you'd be amazed at what is possible."

Do not talk like this.

Nobody.

Talks.

Like.

That.

Example of sounding like a self-help book in the first-person voice:

"I remember struggling with self-doubt, but I have learned to love myself and that has made all the difference. The greatest potential for transformation happens when we can give ourselves compassion."

Okay, yeah. Vulnerability? Check! Relatable story? Check. Good copy, right?

Except not. I just fell asleep writing that shit!

You still sound like a boring ass self-help book. Except in first person.

Here's how you talk:

"When I was hiding in the bathroom at my own sister's baby shower, I knew that shit had hit the fan. I could hear everyone looking for me. I was like, 'OMG, what now?'"

Now I'm listening!

Be human.

Don't put on a "coach-y" voice.

Do not, under any circumstances, sound like a self-help book.

PERFECTION IS UNNECESSARY

If your thing has ONE idea, ONE question, ONE sentence that could help someone, it's worth it.

THEY DON'T WANT TO PROCESS THEIR DAMN EMOTIONS

Don't tell people, "I'll teach you how to process emotions."

Nobody who is not already a mindset coach ever got out of bed and thought to themselves, "Hmm, I am having some emotions to process today."

They think, "My life sucks. I need cookies."

QUANTITY CREATES QUALITY

Want to know what works?

Be willing to do what doesn't work 100 times.

Be willing to write at the B- level — wordy, jargon-y, clunky, boring — the first 1,000 times.

I'm an amazing copywriter *because* I wrote bad copy five thousand times in order to learn what works.

These principles I outlined will save you so much time.

But for you to find your own unique voice and to use these principles with finesse, you have to *practice* putting them to use.

Write today and post.

Write tomorrow and post.

Write the day after that and post.

Post.

Post.

Post.

IT SHOULD MAKE YOU CRINGE

James Altucher said, "If it's not making you cringe a little, it's probably a low-impact post."

NEVER TELL YOUR AUDIENCE

If you know how to give them something that makes them think, "This is so good," you don't have to say it.

Never tell them, "This work will change your life."

Give them something that actually does change their life in a very small, concrete, specific way today.

Never tell them, "You can have more joy in your life."

Give them something that makes their hearts well up with a little joy RIGHT NOW.

SAY IT IN YOUR OWN WORDS

In so much of our copy, we talk about concepts that we learned from our teachers.

Ask yourself this one question: if I were to explain it entirely in my own words, how would I say it?

PERFECT WORDS DON'T MATTER

Having the perfect words doesn't actually matter. There is no such thing as perfect words, anyway.

The quality of your thoughts, your energy, and the value you provide is what will create business.

We work on bettering our copy not because words make or break you, but because it helps us to sharpen our thoughts.

It helps us to think at a higher level. It helps us to clearly communicate our energy and value. It works like a compass or a good radio.

But it is not THE thing.

YOU are the thing.

So don't drive yourself crazy.

BREAKING RULES DOESN'T MATTER

You can write "bad" copy that breaks all of my "rules" and still make a fuckton of money.

Get out there, speak, and serve.

RECORD AND TRANSCRIBE

Ask a good friend that you trust to ask you a question about your product or service. Then answer it. To them. Have a conversation.

It's okay and normal if you get a little tongue-tied at first. Give yourself time to find the flow. Record the whole thing. Transcribe your answer and edit it.

I guarantee that's some of the best-converting copy you could come up with.

It will sound like you. It will be true. It will work.

YOUR VOICE IS NOT LOST IN THE WOODS

Stop trying to *find* your voice. It's not out there, lost in the woods.

Your voice is *created* through large volumes of garbage writing. Earn it.

WRITING COPY DOES NOT TAKE TIME

Writing copy doesn't take time.

Trying to make sure it's *good* and trying to manipulate readers' responses takes time.

BAD COPY EVERY DAY

If you let yourself create one *bad* piece of copy a day, and treat it as an experiment, it's not that your *writing* abilities will improve by the end of this month, though they will.

But *your brain* will change.

You will have a different brain.

A more creative brain.

A more playful, intuitive, original brain.

A brain much less vulnerable to the dictatorship of perfectionism overall, waiting for you at the month's end.

Keep underachieving, friends.

IT'S NOT SUPPOSED TO BE EASY

Nailing down your own copy is not *supposed* to be easy and intuitive.

If it were, copywriting-for-hire would not be an entire giant industry. Think about it!

Professional copywriters get paid good money because their skill is rare and valuable and hard-won.

Beating yourself up that copy is *so hard* and *so painful* is like beating yourself up that your dancing looks nothing like J.Lo's after only a month of practice!

The good news is, you do not need to be at J.Lo's level to win over your people.

You can totally sign all the clients with the copy you can write *now*.

Your belief and energy will carry you and more than make up for the gaps in copy perfection, I promise.

Keep learning and practicing and improving.

But for the love of God, no hand-wringing and saying mean things to yourself because what you can produce now isn't living up to your ideals of perfection.

You're working on developing a serious skill.

It takes work, it takes time, and it will pay you back for the rest of your life.

FEEL FIRST, THEN WRITE

If you find yourself thinking, *I don't even know what to write*, stop thinking. It's hard to think your way out of that, because, more often than not, the emotion underneath thoughts like that is pressure and obligation!

Instead, see if you can try to shift to a different emotion.

Emotions that are conducive to writing include:

- Wonder
- Curiosity
- Appreciation
- Excitement
- Commitment
- Passion
- Devotion
- Interest
- Loving
- Openness
- Connection

Change the way you *feel* first, and everything else will follow.

CLICHÉS ARE A COP-OUT

Speaking in life coach clichés and fluffy concepts are a symptom of you not being confident in your coaching.

It's a hell of a lot easier to say, "I help you create an abundant and peaceful relationship with money," than to say, "I'll help you pay down all your debt and put a heft chunk of change away for a 'fuck you' fund."

Because then you'd have to actually deliver on that.

You'd have to think a lot harder and have a way higher standard for your own coaching and for your clients.

And it's a lot easier to say, "I help you feel more confident and empowered at work," than to say, "I'll help you negotiate a higher salary and *get* it in 4 months."

Because then you'd have to actually deliver on that.

You'd have to think a lot harder and have a way higher standard for your own coaching and for your clients.

Life coach clichés are a cop-out.

Offer a result you'd be proud to deliver on. Up the ante for yourself. What else are we even doing?

We're in the business of creating breakthroughs.

LOW ENGAGEMENT-CREATING COPY

One of the biggest mistakes I see people making is asking the reader to think about far-too-advanced concepts. This results in low engagement.

What you think is a basic coaching principle is far too advanced for most.

Example: "What lies between you and your goal is an unmade decision."

Always ask yourself: Would this have made perfect, immediate clear sense to you 5 years ago?

If not, it's too advanced. You have to bring it down to the "talking to an 8-year-old" level. Nobody has a clue what you mean.

———

What feels like a useful coaching question is far too advanced for most.

Example: "What is the emotion driving your current action?"

Remember, "civilians" do not think in terms of emotions driving actions. They have probably never thought about emotions in an intentional way.

Hence, they cannot answer. Their brains don't compute. They scroll past.

––––––

Nobody's liking or answering your post because nobody has any idea how to process what you're telling them.

You've got to be curious about how to say things in a simpler way.

NOT WORTH IT IF YOU'RE NOT LEARNING

Copy is worth nothing if you're not *learning* from the process.

If you're not actively evaluating, trying different things, tweaking things, gathering data, and forming hypotheses and testing them and iterating based on new knowledge, you're, um, "wasting your garbage."

Let it turn all your garbage posts into nutritious compost that helps your business bloom!

The way you do it is through learning and intentional experimenting, rather than thoughtlessly doing the same thing over and over.

TALK ABOUT CONCRETE RESULTS

Getting away from abstractions and flowery ideas isn't hard. It is not complicated. There's no need to make it so grandiose.

Here's how. Take a look.

Airy fairy: "I will help you to tap into the joy and enthusiasm you've long forgotten."

Concrete: "You'll actually start knitting again. You'll start taking your dogs out for longer walks.

Airy fairy: "I help people to dissolve depression and connect to themselves again."

Concrete: "I'll help you get out of bed in the morning."

Airy fairy: "My art is a representation of the qualities I want people to awaken in themselves."

Concrete: "This painting will give you something to smile about every time you look at the wall. Even if your boss just sent you a bitchy email."

———

Airy fairy: "I help you re-align your relationship with money."

Concrete: "Take the dread out of looking at your bank balance."

DRAMA ABOUT PAST OUTPUT

Regretting or having *ugh* thoughts about past output is poison for your future output.

You keep strengthening the idea that somehow it's possible to *get it wrong*.

That will forever keep you anxious and paranoid and in self-doubt and using only a fraction of your creativity and personal power *trying to get it right*.

Why not decide that you're going to be proud of everything you share, period?

This is what I mean by *deciding to believe I am valuable.*

Every time you show up, you bring value. Period.

Every time you show up, it is good for the world. Period.

Hence, there is no such thing as *did it wrong*. It is logically incompatible with *I have value.*

End of story.

This will free up so much mental space and magnetism.

STOP BABYSITTING ALREADY-
PUBLISHED CONTENT

Wanna know how to create HOURS of time in your week?

Stop babysitting your already-published content.

Babysitting = looking after it, ruminating over it, minding the reactions to it, hovering over it, fretting to see if it's well-liked or at the very least not misunderstood, defending it, debating it, regretting it, testing it, or telling yourself endless stories about it.

Once it's out, it's out.

It's like a kid who grows up and moves out of the house. You don't wanna run after it anymore! No more babysitting!

When you're done sharing, go right back to thinking and imagining the next thing. Keep yourself moving.

If you do this, you'll be unstoppable.

AUTHENTICITY AND INTEGRITY

YOU'RE THE ONE I'VE BEEN WAITING FOR

Business is exactly like dating.

Unlike how it looks, most of the work that contributes to *success* is internal.

Figuring out: who are you? No, who are you REALLY?

What. Do. You. Want?

Are you solid on all that? (If you haven't done the work to get solid on that, you will struggle with both love and business.)

Then you just show up. And be as authentically and powerfully "you" as you can possibly stand.

You're not pitching, you're not manipulating, you're not convincing, you're not supplicating (blech!!!)

You're looking for people who already want you. It's so efficient.

And when they see you, there's that recognition.

"Ahhh! Where have you been? You're the one I've been waiting for."

YOU CAN'T THINK YOUR WAY TO AUTHENTICITY

If you're trying to THINK your way through how to be more authentic on social media, that's like trying to figure out how to give your partner the *hawt sex* by thinking about it.

If you're thinking about it, you're doing it wrong.

Can you be here, now?

Can you, just for this moment, relax all the *shoulds* and suspend your agenda?

Can you open yourself up — just as you are — to be appreciated?

Can you allow yourself to feel safe in the presence of other humans here?

Can you be warmly curious about the person next to you?

BEING AUTHENTIC IS LEARNED

Being authentic is a learned skill.

Isn't that surprising?

I think I got to learn how to find my true voice by trying on other people's voices first, the first 700 times.

Depending on who my teacher or mentor was at the time, everything I said probably ended up sounding like them.

It wasn't intentional copying. It was just that the imprint of their style was so strong on my mind that I unconsciously mimicked their voice. When I tried to speak as *me*, it would just come off awkward or whiny or boring and banal or just not any kind of interesting or inspiring.

My engagement showed it, too.

But I kept practicing and experimenting.

I noticed the subtle differences in energy when I was thinking certain thoughts versus others when writing. I tried copy tactics that *experts* recommended, and noticed which ones actually worked and felt aligned, and which ones just felt gross. Like when you're playing a musical instrument, I experimented with different ways to layer in tension, relief, intensity, and humor into my writing.

I didn't like the result of the bulk of those experiments.

But that's how I found out what I *do* like, what does feel good and like *me*, and what *serves* my friends the most.

I had to sound *wrong* 97 times so that I could figure it out on the 98th try.

After this entire process that took many years, people finally started to tell me that I have a unique voice online.

My friends, keep paying attention. Keep trying stuff! And drop that perfectionism! Have mercy on yourself!

You can have fun because not nailing it every time is exactly the process of becoming someone who does.

LET THEM FEEL TRIGGERED

It is the ultimate act of love to allow people to have the experience of feeling triggered by you without rushing to people-please from an insincere place or making it mean something about your ego.

FUCK BEING A BRAND

Fuck being a *brand*. Who you are, in your full humanity, is the brand.

The beauty of this approach is that when you evolve, your *brand* can evolve with you.

When you grow and pivot, the *brand* naturally does with you. And it all adds up to a coherent story.

THE QUICKEST WAY TO TRANSFORM
YOUR MARKETING

Your marketing will transform the minute you declare yourself radically available for the emotions that come with being ignored or judged.

Decide that you've reached the point where the pain of rejecting yourself is greater than the pain of being rejected by others.

So speak. Let your tender truths meet the world. You will be rewarded in proportion to your courage.

Know this: none of this is mandatory. There's no damn *should*.

You don't need to market this way to be a good person. Or even to be *successful*.

You get to. The opportunity to speak your truth and make a living is a privilege — one that is available to you if you choose it.

There's a profound difference.

YOU SHOULD POST THAT UNPOPULAR OPINION

You should post the unpopular or provocative opinion.*

Because, even if people don't agree with you, they'll respect you more (often, subconsciously) for having the courage to stand your own damn ground.

We all gravitate toward courage.

Some people would call this *positioning yourself as a leader.*

* Post unpopular or provocative opinions, but only if it follows the 3 Rules of Sharing: it is loving**, it is true, and it may be of service to at least one person.

** Loving doesn't necessarily mean positive vibes or warm and fuzzy.

YOUR POSITIONING

Positioning isn't something contrived from a focus group.

Positioning is who you already are at your most powerful and loving.

LYING TO AVOID INTIMIDATING PEOPLE

If you try to make any part of your life appear less beautiful, less joyful, less successful, less prosperous, or less competent than it actually is, in an attempt to avoid intimidating people?

That is literally lying.

It's the same kind of lie as exaggerating your life in order to impress people.

It's being dishonest about who you really are in order to control people's opinions about you.

It's people-pleasing.

Be yourself and let other people have whatever thoughts they want about you.

If you're amazingly competent, show us the truth.

If you're actually impressive, impress.

If you're shiny, shine.

If someone's own story of smallness rubs up against them, that is not your growth to tend to.

It's theirs.

Let them have it.

DO IT HOWEVER YOU WANT

If you charge a lot, you're greedy. If you charge a little, you don't know your worth.

If you say it directly, you're pushy. If you say it indirectly, you're being manipulative.

If you post a lot, you're too much. If you post a little, you're invisible.

If you're assertive, you're a bitch. If you're gentle, you're a wallflower.

Well...

Someone's always gonna have a problem with what you're doing.

Can't please everyone.

So you might as well market however the fuck you want.

STOP DILUTING

When you stop diluting your own personality, edges, and truths, clients chase you, not the other way around.

In my clients and colleagues, I see some patterns happen consistently. When people stop editing themselves, first, they get a bunch of unsubscribes and unfollows.

Then, they make a whole bunch of money.

Every. Single. Damn. Time.

Stop watering yourself down.

Just come out and say the thing.

Dare to offend and disappoint.

IF YOU'RE FIERY

If you're a fiery person and some people aren't feeling the burn in how you show up to market and sell, you're editing yourself down and, as a result, your best clients can't find you and give you money.

If you're fire, your heat, the burn, the scorch — administered with love — *is* the medicine.

If you tamp it down as to not *trigger* or *offend*, you're not helping as much as you can.

DARE TO PIVOT IN PUBLIC

There is no shame in pivoting and iterating in public, over and over. Keep growing and don't be afraid to show up as you wish to be right now.

Who cares if you change your mind later? There's no fucking consistency police.

DON'T REJECT YOURSELF

Don't reject yourself preemptively to save yourself the discomfort of being rejected by others.

What would you do if you weren't preemptively rejecting yourself, your offer, your gifts?

DO YOUR WORK FIRST

Do *your* work first.

If you think meeting your own goals is optional, so will your audience. And they won't invest in coaching, because, eh, it doesn't really matter.

If you think you're confused about what your next step is, so is your audience. And they won't decide to take the next step to invest in coaching.

If you're not investing in getting the help you need because you think you should be able to figure it out on your own, they won't, either. And they won't seek help from you.

If you blame past coaches and programs for *not getting you results*, so do they, and they'll think you're just another investment that won't work out for them, even if they think you're great.

If you're cynical about coaching, so are they.

If you think coaching is a luxury, so do they.

Your clients are not investing in you for the exact reason you're not showing up for your own growth.

THE RESPONSES YOU GET REFLECT
YOUR MONEY MINDSET

If you're trying to extract all the value out of all the content you can from your favorite coaches' resources, and you're just trying to stretch it as far as you can so you don't have to spend money, that's exactly what your prospective clients are doing.

It's not that you have to spend money to make money.

It's that your money mindset is being reflected in the kind of responses you get.

Your lack of belief in your ability to create a great return on your investments does *not* inspire your prospective clients that *they* could.

BE WILLING TO DISAPPOINT

Who are you willing to disappoint today in order to be in integrity with what your business wants to create in the world?

PRIORITIZE THE INSIDE

Being conventionally attractive on the outside can buy you a ton of romantic attention, but your relationship to yourself on the inside will determine whether you get real love.

Executing all the conventional marketing strategies and slapping on shiny *branding* on the outside can buy you a ton of attention, but your relationship to yourself on the inside will determine whether you get real profit.

ACKNOWLEDGMENTS

I owe a gargantuan debt of gratitude to the teachers in my lineage who directly shaped my marketing philosophy and worldview and breathed into me the language of love and service as it applies to business: Stacey Boehman, Brooke Castillo, Fabeku Fatunmise, Havi Brooks, and Melissa Tiers.

Big thanks to Deena Rutter for the beautiful cover and always to my sister Julie Hutchison for being a tireless champion of my writing.

ABOUT THE AUTHOR

Simone Seol is a life coach and business mentor based in Seoul, South Korea. She hosts the Joyful Marketing podcast and works with coaches all over the world to create a revolution in love-based marketing.

ALSO BY SIMONE SEOL

Don't Do Your Best: A Guide to the Project of Being Alive

I can have a week where one day I'm bawling my eyes out + the next day I'm strong up + enjoying the energy.

both are fine. both are me. I give myself permission to feel both. the crying doesn't make me 'broken'. The energy doesn't make me 'better'. They both just make me me

Things I've seen people struggling with this week.

Stop outsourcing your feelings

- to an algorithm
- to how someone else talks to you
- to your expectations of how things 'should' be

You are giving away all of your power.
Please don't

I work with people who are tired of feeling like their brain is working against them

Printed in Great Britain
by Amazon